The
Teachable
Moment

The
Teachable
Moment

Seizing the Instants When Children Learn

Rebecca Branstetter, Editor

KAPLAN

PUBLISHING

New York

Published by Kaplan Publishing, a division of Kaplan, Inc.
1 Liberty Plaza, 24th Floor
New York, NY 10006

Printed in the United States of America

10 9 8 7 6 5 4 3 2 1

Library of Congress Cataloging-in-Publication Data has been applied for.

ISBN-13: 978-1-4277-9967-8

Kaplan Publishing books are available at special quantity discounts to use for sales promotions, employee premiums, or educational purposes. For more information or to purchase books, please call the Simon & Schuster special sales department at 866-506-1949.

Contents

INTRODUCTION: THE HARVEST

I BLAME MICHELLE PFEIFFER and I blame Robin Williams. I blame them for making teaching look so easy in their movies and giving me a false sense of confidence as an educator. When I first started out in the public schools, I thought all you needed was a good heart and the children would follow. Sure, there would be the first half-hour in which you had to gain the students' trust, but as soon as they saw how much you cared, they would be raising their hands appropriately and making connections, and their love of learning would shine though.

And then I tried to conduct a classwide discussion about a serious topic in a sixth-grade middle school classroom in a large urban school district in the San Francisco Bay Area.

I am actually a school psychologist, not a teacher. If a teacher and a psychologist had a baby, that baby would be a school psychologist. We seek to understand what motivates kids to learn, what gets in the way of learning, and how to help teachers and parents work better with kids. My training was geared toward the "Show you care and they will follow!" mantra. Most of my experience involves observing teachers' and students' interactions, pulling out the "troubled" kid, having a nice one-on-one discussion about what is going on, and shipping the kid back to class. Later I check back in with the teacher about what is really going on for the student, and we develop a plan.

Oh, but I have had my fair share of "tough" kids who show up with a scowl, dressed in army fatigues, armed with their defenses and long-standing history of being misunderstood. Within the first half hour, the Michelle Pfeiffer tough-love strategy usually works. I have seen a 10-year-old girl who had, moments before, cursed out a teacher (in language not suitable to repeat in a book on the teachable moment) turn into a giggling sweetheart. I have seen a giant, surly adolescent morph into a sweet young man who admits he loves poetry. I have seen a shy girl finally speak after a year of silence, all by the power of listening, validating, and trying to understand where they are coming from.

However, my first time outside the world of positive one-on-one interactions with kids, in the realm of the classroom, was most unfortunate. I arrived at my middle school that day, like any other day, lugging my materials in a rolling bag, like a flight attendant, because there was no space to give me an office at this school. As I rolled in, the principal frantically waved me into her office, where two policemen and the vice principal stood with furrowed brows and a sense of urgency.

"Rebecca, I'm going to need you to go to all the sixth-grade classes and do a debriefing on a few incidents. First, Michael's father was shot and killed last night."

"Oh, my God. That's awful. What happened?"

"He was in the wrong place at the wrong time and got hit during a drive-by. Michael saw the whole thing."

"Wow. Poor Michael . . . wait. Did you say a *few* incidents?"

My principal sighed and said, "Yes. Mrs. X was arrested yesterday for sleeping with a sixth-grade boy and will no longer be teaching here. She is in jail and the boy is here today."

Right. Got it. I'm on it. The only problem was that at that time, I was a 23-year-old intern school psychologist, equipped only with idealism and the training to work with kids one-on-one. Surely I could talk to a whole class, though? I had observed many veteran teachers work their magic. My mother and sister were excellent teachers. I had read extensively on theories of teaching and learning, classroom management, and psychology. Plus I had given oodles of excellent teaching advice to teachers through consultation. Through osmosis I had probably learned how to do a lesson in front of 30 kids on dealing with a crisis, right?

As I tried to process all that information at once,

I started to rack my brain: when had they taught this particular situation in graduate school at Berkeley? I think we had a class on crisis management . . . Where were those handouts? The only thing I could remember was that you needed to deliver a clear, honest message to the students, and if you don't know the answer, say so. I dropped off my giant bag in the principal's office, grabbed some markers and paper, and headed to the first class. Armed only with adrenaline and my one course in crisis management, I mentally rehearsed how to tell a classroom of students that their friend has lost his dad to the all-too-familiar community violence and that their teacher is a pedophile. I ran over all the worst-case scenarios in my head and concluded that if I got in a pinch the teacher would help me out, because he had experience in communicating on a classroom level.

If I could do it all over, I would have stopped for a second and called my supervisor for advice, but I wanted to show that I was capable. I was Superpsychologist. I had a lesson plan, carefully crafted in my head in the time it took to walk from the principal's office to my first classroom of sixth-grade students.

As I entered the classroom, I heard murmurs from the 11- and 12-year-olds.

"Is Michael here today?"

"My dad got shot once too."

"I heard Mrs. X got arrested!"

"I think they were in love though."

I took a deep breath and did as I was told. I first presented the facts, as I knew them, about Michael's father. The kids already knew. One girl asked if we could make cards for Michael's family, and we agreed as a class to do just that. I passed out the paper and markers and they got right to work. I circulated about the room and checked in with each student individually about his or her thoughts and feelings about the shooting. Sadly, many were so used to this type of violence they seemed, at least on the outside, nonplussed. Over the years they had already learned to cope with losing family and friends to community violence. I made mental notes of all the kids who brought up how they had lost someone recently, to do follow-up meetings. I knew that new traumas could spark painful memories of past traumas. So far, things were going along well. I was nervous, however, about the next step.

After I gathered up the beautiful cards for Michael, full of rainbows, crosses, and "I'm sorry's," I took another deep breath. The class was not focused on me at all. They started popping up out of their seats as in that carnival game where those little plastic moles pop up out of their holes, while I futilely tried to pop them back down with my words.

"I need you to have a seat, Keisha. Thank you . . . Jasmine, can you please be seated? Right, um, you there, take your seat."

Finally, when my soft one-on-one approach failed,

the teacher shouted, "Sit down if you want to hear about the situation with Mrs. X." If there had been a record playing, it would have scratched to silence at that point, and all the kids sat down quietly, facing forward at attention. I then explained the facts about their teacher, being careful to not say who the student was, even though everyone probably knew. I explained what reactions they might have, from a psychological perspective—confusion, anger, sadness, numbness, the whole deal. I thought I explained myself pretty darn well, in kid-friendly language. I mentally patted myself on the back.

It was at that point that a boy stood up on his desk and started humping the air, to express his thoughts on the matter. The class erupted into laughter as I sank into my own personal hell. I immediately flashed to that scene in *Dead Poets Society* in which all the kids stand triumphantly on their chairs in support of the teacher. This was not the standing-on-the-chair moment I was hoping for.

This was also the big decision point. I could reprimand the boy and potentially lose the whole class. I could ignore him and continue, and the implicit lesson would be that gyrating in a crisis is perfectly acceptable. I panicked and looked at the teacher for help. He suddenly became enthralled with something on his sleeve. Thanks, buddy. Thankfully, the teachable-moment goddess smiled upon me and I said, "Frankie has just demonstrated another possible way to deal with difficult situations—by using humor." The class stopped laughing, Frankie got down off his desk, several kids nodded in agreement, and we pressed forward.

From that day to this, I never give teaching advice without first acknowledging how hard teaching is and how there are no straightforward "answers" when it comes to reaching each student. I look back now and laugh at how naïve I was and how I should have relied on my colleagues for support. Years later, I now have a whole bag of tricks for difficult teaching moments, tricks that I have learned not from my zillions of graduate-school readings but from my fellow educators.

This is what this collection of essays on the teachable moment is all about. Teachers across the country have written about the moments that transformed their students and their own teaching. True to life, and not too Hollywood, these tales capture the subtle, incremental, and unpredictable moments in teaching. Rare is the moment in which a teacher sees an immediate, direct payoff for all his or her hard work, planning, and consistency in the classroom. In a standards-based climate that fixates on measuring growth by yearly tests, I still believe that teaching is mostly a faith-based profession.

Each day, the teacher plants a seed, nurtures it, and hopes other environmental conditions will be favorable to growth. Then the teacher patiently waits and continues planting and watering new seeds. The teacher never knows which seed will sprout first or how fast.

Sometimes it feels like pouring water into sand, because you can't see the growth right away. The moments when you instantly transform your students, à la Michelle Pfeiffer and Robin Williams, are rare. Teachers must judge each day not by the harvest but by the seeds they plant in each child. Because every so often, along comes the harvest, when the students let the teacher know they got it. At long last, the fruits of the teacher's labor are finally tangible, and so sweet. It's the harvest that keeps us going. Enjoy.

—Rebecca Branstetter, PhD

◼

SECTION ONE

IN SEARCH OF
THE ACADEMIC "AHA!"

Teaching Is Hard

Mrs. Mimi
(as created by Jennifer Scoggin)

T EACHING IS HARD. Even rock-star teachers, like myself, need something to cling to when the administrative and other outside nonsense starts to seep under the door of our classrooms, threatening to render us insane or completely ineffective. We begin to float away from our responsibilities and ideals on a sea of bullshit so deep and so wide that sometimes it seems we will never make our way back to school again. Imagine me, clinging desperately to my Sharpies® and Post-it® notes as a sea of classroom interruptions washes over me, robbing me of any ability or desire to keep going. It's a sad, sad sight, isn't it? But we've all been there.

And in those dark moments, I have found that my little second-grade friends are the ones who come to my rescue. There are the days when I look around my classroom and see 20 little life jackets looking back at me. They may not be aware of it (and they can certainly drive me crazy on other days), but somehow they know just what to say a moment before I drown.

The scene: Harlem, 2007. It's a rainy Wednesday in March. Nineteen children sit anxiously on the carpet, visibly leaning forward to hear the genius issue from my lips. OK, so maybe *they* wouldn't call it genius, but I've never been shy about tooting my own horn, and at least they were trying to be attentive. What about friend number twenty? Well, that's my little Muppet. And he is definitely not anxiously awaiting anything besides recess.

Now, Muppet is one of the cutest students I have ever had. For real. He is super-mini, with big brown eyes, and this insanely curly hair that is always either totally out of control or braided into slick cornrows. I'm not sure which look I like better. Either way, Muppet reminds me very much of a Dr. Seuss character. (I thought about calling him Thing One, but that's not very nice, so Muppet it is.) In addition to being unbelievably cute, Muppet is kind to other children, sweet to me, and helpful around the classroom. I know, Muppet sounds almost too good to be true. But don't worry, 'cause here comes the other shoe. (It's dropping hard and fast.) Muppet is reading almost an entire year below grade level and is a total space cadet. So yes, he is super-cute, but totally out to lunch!

Earlier that morning, I am working with Muppet in a small group while everyone else is (allegedly) reading silently. He is sitting right in front of my face and still blatantly refusing to listen. I'm talking, and his eyes are everywhere but my face. I ask him to read out loud, and all of a sudden his eyes are all over my face, instead of the page, as if the correct word were going to magically appear to him on my forehead. Getting Muppet to love reading, and to listen when I'm talking about reading, has been difficult all year, but today takes our struggle to new heights. This is a child who will volunteer to help clean up the messiest of art projects, but ask him to read a book? Perish the thought! I am about to resort to my Jerry Maguire-esque "Help Me Help You" speech when I decide that this is not the week I am going to win over Muppet. Instead, I just send him back to his seat with a book.

Sigh.

It had been a rough week all around and it really wasn't the fault of my little friends. Let's see, so far that week my teaching had been interrupted roughly five to six times a day, which works out to about once an hour. Yeah, that's about eighteen different interruptions altogether and it was only Wednesday! These interruptions came in many forms. There was the ever-popular school phone call interruption in which the person on the other end inevitably has the wrong classroom or nothing important to say and yet manages to convey this to me in the rudest of possible tones.

Me: (midsentence, watching as the ringing of the phone visibly causes every student on the rug to disengage) Hello?

Interrupter: (in very rude tones) Whose room is this?

Me: (*Didn't you call me?*) Mrs. Mimi's.

Interrupter: Oh. Never mind. (*Slam!*)

Me: (*sigh*) Where were we? Anyone? Anyone? Hel-looo? . . .

Then we had the equally popular "pop-in." During a pop-in some person (usually one of the many, many people who, for reasons I don't understand, have far too little to do during school hours) pops into my classroom, swinging open the door with such force that it literally rips our learning in half. *Bang!* Of course, at this point, the popper asks me (read: shouts in an inappropriate voice across my classroom) something that could easily have been handled via email or a note in my mailbox.

And finally, we have the intercom, a source of endless interruptions. Ironically, these interruptions always start with the phrase "Pardon the interruption." But after several nonsensical and unnecessary interruptions in a row, they become increasingly difficult to pardon.

Notice I am referring mostly to the interruptions made by other adults. These adults are hired as "support staff" (please notice the very intentional use of quotation marks); they are theoretically supposed to support the work of teachers. In reality, I get more support from a bra. Do the kids ever interrupt our learning? Sure they do. But they are seven or eight years old, and their misbehavior is to be expected from time to time. I signed up to deal with their shenanigans. Now, the shenanigans (read: bullshit) that I take from other adults? Intolerable.

These incessant interruptions totally blow my little friends' focus. I mean, kids were trying to get away with all sorts of crap that, on a better week, would seem unthinkable. But this week, oh this week, it was like taking a giant step back to the first month of school, or as I like to call it the "let's see how far we can push her" stage. Ah, memories . . .

Needless to say, teaching was virtually impossible. My usual silent readers' workshop now sounded more like Grand Central Station at rush hour. I must have asked each individual friend, "Are you making a smart choice right now?" at least a hundred times. And the answer was no, they were not making smart choices. Particularly Muppet.

Enough complaining. I'm sure at this point you have a fairly clear reason why I might regularly have the desire to run screaming from the building. You're probably thinking to yourself right this minute, "Self, throw this woman a life raft!"

Because this is about the kids, right? The kids and those moments that make me come back day after day, despite all the administrative and organizational brouhaha, and actually utter the words "I love my job" in public.

Because I do love my job.

So, in the face of all things ridiculous, I try very hard to stay positive when I am in front of my friends. Because I love them. I sometimes imagine myself as the proverbial fence—you know, the one with the greener grass on the other side? (If you can't tell already, I loves me a good metaphor. Stick with me. This is a good one.) Well, I'm the actual fence. On one side of me, there are mountains of administrative bullshit, some of which is literally sliding down the side of me into steaming piles; while on the other side of me, my friends run around in the green grass. As the fence, it is my job to keep one side away from the other. And on a lucky day, my friends come and rescue me right back.

I have taught for eight years. Every single class has worked their way into my heart and come together as a little family by the middle of the year. I say the middle of the year because the beginning of the year is rough on everyone. In September we are all still in summer mode, myself included. (And any teacher who doesn't admit that September is filled with exciting possibilities but also colored by an intense longing for those carefree days of August is lying.) Mr. Mimi says I go through the same stages every year. He might also add that these stages are filled with intense drama and self-doubt, but whatever. He says I'm overdramatic, but I say I make our life more interesting. So, according to Mr. Mimi, I make my way through the predictable stage of Apprehension and Anxiety (also known as September), during which I worry about my incoming group of friends and the upcoming school year. I often find myself handling this stress through endless and obsessive list-making. Then I move into Uncertainty and Loss (also known as October) as I begin to truly miss my friends from the previous year and the easy rapport that we had developed with each other. Finally, I find myself in a Comfortable Routine (November through the end of the year) with my new group of friends, who start to feel more like a family away from our families.

This makes me one lucky woman. Seriously. I don't know many teachers who haven't had that "class from hell" that shakes them to the depths of their educational core. But I haven't. Not yet at least. Sometimes though it feels as if I am just waiting for the other shoe to drop. And that year, I was beginning to think of Muppet and our little battle of wills over reading as that other shoe.

So how did I get this lucky? I could give you some ridiculous rote list of Ten Easy Steps to a New and Improved Classroom Community that would most likely end in one of two ways: A) You think I am far too full of myself and don't make it past Brilliant Idea Number Five, or B) I run the risk of reducing teaching to a list of prescriptive steps that are guaranteed to work every time. I am not willing to take either risk.

What I will tell you is that I spend a lot of time finding new ways to build up my little friends, gain their trust, and show them I truly care about them. Last month my Love Fest du Jour was all about "spying" on my friends to catch them doing kind things for one another. When I caught them in an act of kindness, I would write it on a huge heart and hang it from the lights on the ceiling. Sounds simple and a bit cheesy, but it works. I don't know why it works, but I learned a long time ago not to question the simple power of stickers and other seemingly obvious motivators.

Now, don't get it twisted, it's not all flowers and sausages in my classroom either. I constantly push my friends to work harder, take more responsibility for their own learning, to *do something!* And while I am busy push, push, pushing away, I try to remember to stop periodically and remind them how smart they really are before I push them right over the edge. We celebrate every academic success no matter how large or small, although I have to admit that I am pretty anti–pizza party or other unrelated celebration. Just like the punishment should fit the crime, I feel like the reward should fit the accomplishment. This means that sometimes the celebration is small and private. For example, there are times when a friend finally does something seemingly insignificant, such as move away from another disruptive child to focus on his own work. At first glance, it appears as if nothing truly spectacular has occurred. But if this is the first time that this friend has taken responsibility for his own learning and made the smart choice to find a better place to focus, in my mind that is unbelievably huge. Am I going to stop everything and whip out my pom-poms? (Yes, I do have pom-poms.) No. The pom-poms stay in the closet for a rainy day. In these moments, sometimes all my little friends seem to need is a small gesture of acknowledgment. So I will quietly saunter over to that smart, proactive friend, take his little face in my hand, and say, "You are so smart. I am proud of you."

Again, I don't question the power of these small things. It's just not worth my time.

This one particular moment of success stands out in my mind as one of the reasons that I teach. I have pulled this memory out, dusted it off, and clung to it more times than I can count. And on that dreary, interruption-filled Wednesday, it truly saved me from drowning.

By March, Muppet had made progress, but it was slow. Painfully slow. For both of us. I had given this kid so many pep talks that I was one pep talk short of whipping out those pom-poms and cheering him on from the side-lines. He received all the extra help I could beg, borrow, and steal. Yet more and more of my friends were graduating to more difficult books, while my Muppet stayed with easy books. Although he never said anything to me, I knew it bugged him to be so far behind. There were days when I noticed him trying to hide his books from the other children at his table because his books were filled with big, colorful pictures and very little text. While his friends blissfully made their way through a chapter book,

Muppet sat staring at the ceiling. Did his embarrassment motivate him to spend more time reading? Of course not, but it did motivate the heck out of me to find what else I could do to help. And while it was tempting to think about taping him to the chair and propping the book up in front of his face, I knew I had to find a more reasonable way to get this kid motivated to read.

That morning I gave up and sent Muppet back to his seat with a book. It was a nonfiction book about octopuses that I knew was on his reading level, but at the time, giving him a nonfiction text was a very random choice. You see, I have a stack of books in my reading area that are organized by level. Usually I just work my way through the stack, caring more about the level of the book than I do about the title or story. Honestly, I just needed to send Muppet away and take a moment to regroup.

Now, feeling guilty, I wander over to his desk to see how he is doing. I am immediately thrown off by what I find: Muppet is totally engrossed in the book, studying each photograph-filled page as if it were pure genius. At his level, there are only two or three sentences on each page, but Muppet is intently working his way through each and every word. I watch him study the page, taking in all the labels and, well, reading.

Me: So, how's it going over here?

Muppet: Mrs. Mimi?

Me: Yes, honey?

Muppet: OK, wait. Wait. Wait. OK, so you're saying that I can read this book and actually learn stuff?

Me: (*Um, what?*) Well, yes. Of course you can.

Muppet: Even me?

Me: Of course even you.

Muppet: So, I can want to know about something, find the book, and teach myself?

Me: Um, yeah. You can absolutely do that. That's what we were talking about today.

Muppet: Cool!

Me: Do you want to know more about anything in particular? I could find some more books for you . . .

Muppet: Really, you would do that?

Me: (*Are you freaking kidding me? I was contemplating taping you to a chair just a few minutes ago . . . and now you're asking me for books? Uh, yeah I'll go get them.*) Of course. Just tell me what you want to learn more about.

Just like that, Muppet decided that while he hated learning how to read, reading to learn was right up his alley. Dude, if only I had figured this out three months ago! I gave him nonfiction book after nonfiction book and he devoured every single one. He read books about animals, books about people, books about places. Almost every day he would be desperate to show me something that he had learned in a book *all by himself!*

A few weeks went by. It was time to reassess my little friends and send my administrators an update on their progress in reading. (You know how those administra-tors love their graphs and charts! Test, test, test!)

It was Muppet's turn to get tested. With a bit of trepidation on my part, I handed him the text to read. Things had been going so well lately, and I didn't want to discourage him in any way, but in the world of schools, a test is An Unavoidable Event and, unfortu-nately, sometimes more important than my instincts or the feelings of one of my friends.

So I gave Muppet the test.

Then I held my breath and listened to him read.

And . . .

(wait for it)

(*wait for it*)

Muppet rocked the test.

Not only did he rock it, he all of a sudden was able to read much more difficult fictional texts and had pride in his newfound reading ability. I looked at Muppet and (restraining myself from dancing on the table) shouted, "Check you out! You did it! You're a reader, friend!"

And then my little Muppet reached across the table, took my face in his hands, and simply said, "Thank you."

ALLEVIATING SHAKES-FEAR

Damian Bariexca

O F ALL THE difficulties I struggled with as a new
teacher, one of the most herculean tasks I faced
was not classroom management or dealing with difficult parents: it was getting my students interested in
Shakespeare. In retrospect, I guess I should have been
able to identify with them a bit more; after all, even as
an honors student and self-professed English geek, I was
nearly through high school before I even began to appre-
ciate his works, and then not until the end of my under-
graduate program did I really start to feel like I could
engage the texts on a level deeper than what my Cliff's
Notes were giving me. The summer after I graduated

from college, I was recruited by my Shakespeare professor to play the role of Young Siward in *Macbeth*. My prior acting experience had been limited to a few high-school musicals, so this was a great first Shakespearean role: I got to say four or five lines, have a short swordfight with Macbeth, and then die (my being "of woman born" my chief liability on the battlefield).

This opportunity led to others within the theater company. Over the next few years, I would play increasingly larger roles in *Henry IV: Part I, The Tempest,* and *A Midsummer Night's Dream*. About midway through this succession of roles, I landed my first full-time position as an English teacher. By that time, I was a bona fide Shakespeare nut and ready to bring my love of the Bard to the unsuspecting 10th graders with whom I'd be covering *Macbeth* that fall.

I think it's safe to say that my first time around teaching Shakespeare to high-school students didn't go *exactly* as planned. For some odd reason, they weren't as excited to be reading the Scottish play as I was, and I was actually met with *resistance* when I told them how great the play was! I struggled through the play with them as best I could as a new teacher, and I think I speak for students and teacher alike when I say that we were all quite relieved when it was over. My first attempt at teaching Shakespeare was, as Will S. himself might have said, a hot mess.

As any teacher does, I picked up little tips and tricks

my second and third time around with the play, and each time it got a little less painful (which is what I was gunning for, really). I was doing passably well with the text once we got rolling, but I was still lacking that "hook" that was going to grab my kids from the outset. I felt it was taking too long to get the kids interested and invested in what was happening (although "by Act III" was much better than my first attempt, which was "not at all"). Fortunately for me (and my students), all I would need is a push in the right direction, and it was about to come.

In the summer of 2002, I was one of 26 teachers from around the United States selected to participate in the Teaching Shakespeare Institute (TSI) in Washington, DC. The TSI, held at the Folger Shakespeare Library every other summer, allows teachers access to the Folger facilities and faculty, as well as to distinguished American Shakespearean scholars, to collaborate on creating exciting and engaging materials for teaching the works of Shakespeare. To expound upon the admiration and respect I have for the people involved in the TSI is beyond the scope of this story, but I mention the creative focus of the institute because this is what jump-started me toward thinking differently about teaching Shakespeare. Ironically enough, however, the hook I'd been seeking for years came to me in the least likely place: a lecture hall.

During one of our introductory lectures, Dr. Robert Watson of UCLA was making a point about the contrast between the romanticized storybook version of the Renaissance period that we often hear about versus the often horrible truths about pestilence, disease, and generally hard living conditions to which the majority of Renaissance England was subject. I remember him using a variation on the phrase "I hate to burst your bubble," and as I was taking a short break from studiously and furiously taking notes, I started doodling a popping balloon. I then began to think about Dr. Watson's point about preconceived notions in the context of teaching Shakespeare, and it occurred to me that so many students fight learning about Shakespeare because *they have already convinced themselves it's going to be awful.* (This may not be news for many of you, but I was still a new teacher, so I was taking all the revelations I could get.)

Over the course of the institute, I worked alongside some incredible teachers, actors, playwrights, and scholars, all of whom helped me come to a better understanding of how to approach Shakespeare with my students; for this, I am indebted to them. When I returned to my classroom in New Jersey the following fall, I took all that with me but remained guided by that initial little flash I had in the lecture hall: *Start strong. Do not let them convince themselves that they can't do this. Do not let them beat themselves before they even start. Don't even give them half a chance.*

My tenth-grade English class started our study of *Macbeth* right around Halloween that year, appropriately enough. This time, rather than try any of my previous opening activities (much of which resulted in the students complaining about how hard "this Old English stuff" was), I had decided that I was going to burst my students' bubbles—or rather, they were going to burst their own.

When my young charges entered the room that day, they saw five red balloons stuck to the whiteboard with tape. Each balloon had taped to it an 8½ × 11 sheet of paper with one of the following phrases printed on it in 100-point type:

- Shakespeare wrote intellectual "high drama."
- The Renaissance was a wonderful time to be alive!
- Shakespeare was highly educated and wrote specifically for kings, queens, and nobility.
- We can learn more about Shakespeare by studying his plays.
- The issues Shakespeare wrote about have no bearing on my world.

I explained to the class that these statements represented some commonly held misconceptions about Shakespeare and Elizabethan England, and that today we were going to symbolically destroy these beliefs that even the very highly educated and refined members of this class themselves may hold. Volunteers would come to the board to read one statement out loud, pop the balloon, and then read aloud the folded-up refutation that I had placed inside the balloon before inflating it.

The initial response was blank stares and silence from the class. Uh-oh. Had I completely lost the plot? Was this too babyish for my high-school sophomores? After what seemed like an eternity of silence (which was roughly equivalent to three seconds real-time), an explosion of "Ooh, me!" and "Can I go first?" and "Mr. B, can I get a shot?" and other general commotion overwhelmed me. When I heard one of my much less motivated students say to himself (unironically), "Wow, that's really creative," I knew it: they were hooked!

Five students got to (not "had to"!) go to the front of the room, pop a balloon, and explain to their classmates about the hygienic pitfalls of living in England during Shakespeare's time, the universality of Shakespeare's themes, and the rather straight lines one can draw between Shakespeare's plays and some modern horror movies. Afterwards I gave every student in the class their very own red balloon, into which I instructed them to channel every bad feeling and negative association they ever had with William Shakespeare. Then, on the count of three, we all popped our balloons in a cathartic release of negative energy.

Of course, a hook without substance is nothing but a cheap gimmick, and to follow a start like that with anything less than both barrels blazing would have been a heartbreaking waste of momentum. So we then did some work with Shakespeare's language and physical movement, just getting familiar with the vocabulary and cadence and simply getting the words into and out of our mouths, much like a baseball player takes a few practice swings before stepping up to bat. A little bit of acting, some discussion about stage directions, unfamiliar syntax, and using context clues to determine meaning, and before I knew it they were arguing over who got to be the witches first in Act 1, Scene 1.

In subsequent years, I added *Hamlet, A Midsummer Night's Dream, Measure for Measure,* and *Twelfth Night* to the list of Shakespearean plays I would explore with my students. While the specific assignments and activities varied by play, I found that by following a few guiding principles I was able to make Shakespeare a relatively painless (possibly even enjoyable!) experience for my students.

While we all had a great time popping balloons and making a commotion, at the heart of that activity was an attempt to help the students get to the content in an unconventional way. Along that line, I've found that having a healthily irreverent attitude toward Shakespeare can go a long way toward defusing some of the anxiety, intimidation, and subsequent resistance students demonstrate when confronted with this seemingly foreign writing. Where others might put Shakespeare up on a pedestal, I always aimed to take him down off the pedestal and have some fun with him. Making jokes and poking fun at odd phrasings or situations had my students laughing with me, and we were all in the Shakespeare boat together, which made for a dynamic well suited to open-mindedness and learning.

Physical movement is imperative to any study of Shakespeare. I cringe when I think of all the time I wasted as a young teacher having students sit in their chairs, reading the play aloud. Having my students get up and move around with the text made them think not just about what is being said but also how that translates into physical action and why. Whenever I asked students to block scenes, I would always challenge them to defend their blocking: why should Juliet stand here instead of there? Why did Ophelia give the flowers to her instead of him? Acting out the same scene in different ways can also lead to high-level discussion about character motivation and major themes in the context of a director's deciding how to stage a scene. For example, I used to split my sophomore classes in half and ask one group to act out the banquet scene from *Macbeth* twice: once with an actor playing the ghost of Banquo, and once with no one playing Banquo. We then discussed how both the audience and Macbeth's dinner guests are impacted by a directorial decision to have Macbeth scream at an actor in ghost makeup versus having him scream at an empty chair. These exercises helped the students gain a more multidimensional understanding of the play—not just what's happening but why, and what could (or could not) happen as a result.

Also in a performance vein, I strongly suggest watching movies with your students. More accurately, I suggest watching clips of movies. I don't believe I ever showed a complete film start to finish during any study of Shakespeare. I used clips of scenes to reinforce basic comprehension or to make a point as needed, but my primary focus was to use film as a text for analysis and discussion. One of my favorite film-based activities was to show three different versions of the same scene in *Hamlet* and have my students discuss whether they felt Mel Gibson, Campbell Scott, or Ethan Hawke had the most accurate take on the great Dane, and why. (They are three very different portrayals.) We also examined how each film treats the relationship between Hamlet and Ophelia, and discussed the major points of contrast and what impact that has on the audience's perspective. Studying how closely different versions of a scene (such as Titania's seduction of Bottom from *A Midsummer Night's Dream*) adhere to the text can lead very easily to discussions of how the tone of a scene (and the subsequent impact on the play) can be altered by omitting a single line or set of lines or by rearranging the events of a scene.

Speaking of lines, editing Shakespeare's text is a fantastic exercise in critical reading. I often gave small groups of students a scene and instructed them to edit out ten (or twenty, or thirty) percent of the lines. To do this effectively, they had to work together to distinguish what was essential to the scene and what was not, as well as what might be important to keep for later in the play. Because I've never been one to ask my students to do something I wouldn't do or haven't done myself; I have done this, and I can honestly say that it is one of the most difficult things I've ever been asked to do with a Shakespeare play. Try it yourself before you assign it to your students; you'll see what I mean.

Regardless of the teaching strategies you try, above all, please: have fun. If you dread teaching Shakespeare, your students will dread learning Shakespeare. If you display your genuine enthusiasm, however, and can maintain a lighthearted attitude, even the most reluctant learners can be brought along for the ride.

AN ODE TO SMALL VICTORIES

Valerie Braimah

I F YOU'RE LIKE me (perhaps old and overly sentimental?), you'll never forget the moment in *Dead Poets Society* when a dozen prep-school boys, having been transformed by their inspired English teacher, Mr. Keating, stand on their desks in a salute to their teacher, chanting Walt Whitman's "O Captain! My Captain!" Since seeing that pivotal scene, I've regularly fantasized about the transformative effect I too could have on the misguided youth of America. Thanks to that moment, we English teachers have visions of the day when our students, so impassioned by the mystical lure of literature, will jump up on their desks, clamoring for their chance to unleash their newfound insight and wisdom. These students, no longer helpless captives of being "cool," can't wait to read, write, speak, and maybe even dream about literature.

I have that vision. I also have several students who, even in 11th grade, are unable to read Walt Whitman, much less mine his symbols to salute my greatness. I knew my *Dead Poets* dream was in peril when my first 10-page reading assignment in *The Autobiography of Malcolm X* (technically an eighth-grade reading level) was met with groans and complaints. "Ten pages? Look how small this print is!" "I saw the movie, does that count?" One of my students went so far as to slam the book down, exclaiming, "You be doin' too much, Ms. Braimah!" OK, so apparently I was going to have to take a couple of steps back and reevaluate my curriculum.

However, watering down my expectations or dumbing down the curriculum were not options: I needed to get my students to proficiency on the 55 complex, wordy, and weighty standards the state requires me to teach. Given the literacy level of many of my students, compounded by the dense, high-level standards I was expected to teach, some might not blame me for being satisfied to pass my students with a decent level of proficiency. But is that really good enough? Would Walt's captain have settled for such meek plunder? If all I did was prepare my class to succeed on standardized tests, I would be falling short of my vision and shortchanging my students, who after 11 years of rote learning and compliance, surely deserve to have the treasures of language and literature unearthed.

Undaunted, I was determined to find a way to make the grade-level content standards my friends and maybe even my allies. In English 11 we are expected to ensure that students can "trace the development of American literature from the colonial period forward," among other things. Faced with the task of introducing my students to *all* American literature from the last 400 years, I wondered if maybe my *Dead Poets Society* moment would have to remain a Hollywood dream. I could already picture Latisha, who reads at a fifth-grade level, attempting to decipher Anne Bradstreet's poetry or draw connections between the Constitution and St. Jean de Crevecoeur. "What's this got to do with me, Ms. Braimah? Why we trippin' over these dead folk?"

As a new teacher, I have been subjected to *many* days of intense training on standards-based planning. As I obligingly examined, unpacked, and prioritized my standards, I started to see where there might be room for creativity, and maybe even inspiration. If students would have to "contrast the major periods, themes, styles, and trends and describe how works by members of different cultures relate to one another in each period," why couldn't I focus on themes and cultures they cared about and topics they would want to read, write, and talk about? Maybe the standards are not simply "over their heads." Maybe there is some way to use the standards as inspiration and then organize them for accessibility. *Surely even a student who cannot read can still be expected to think?*

Finally, I was able to develop a curriculum that I felt sure would inspire avid discussion, critical thinking, and passionate debate. My students would be using American literature to explore themes of race, gender, immigration, justice, and oppression. They would be analyzing political rhetoric, forming and defending their positions, and becoming the informed voters and leaders of tomorrow.

With this vision and my engaging theme-based curriculum in hand, bright eyes shining and bushy tail wagging, I eagerly met my students for the first time. "Teachable moment," I thought, "here I come!" Knowing that we would be delving into controversial, sometimes very personal issues, I cleverly decided to open the class with some icebreakers and team-builders to create a comfortable environment for honest sharing. I imagined students exploring their commonalities, revealing their uniqueness, and developing a deeper appreciation for each other's differences. As it turned out, they would look at me like I was crazy, pull their hoods over their heads (literally and figuratively), and divulge the minimum amount necessary to "get this class over with." Right, so maybe you do need to do more than lead a horse to water. But how could I make them drink?

It turns out that inspiring the youth of America is a

slow, arduous process, and that the results are rarely the kinds of climactic events Robin Williams might have us believe. Three units into the year, I was still waiting for my hero's welcome. To be fair, I have yet to stand on a desk, wear costumes, or yell "Carpe diem!" or "Yop!" Yet I am encouraged by the small victories as I see the students begin to open up, begin to think, begin to challenge me and each other.

I am moved when Thomas, who barely spoke in *my* class, tells me that he is a vocal participant in his diversity class because "we already did that stuff in English, so I know the 4-1-1." Could it be that my class was just planting the seed for Thomas? Will he go on to really tackle some of those social issues? I was inspired when Artan asked why the colonists were able to land on American soil and simply call themselves American, while his Honduran friend has been trying for 15 years to get a green card. These are the seedlings of intellectual curiosity, the early buds of critical thought.

Heroism in the classroom is not a miraculous moment. Rather, it is a painstaking process that begins with great planning and requires relentless persistence. My students, afraid to be seen as "schoolboys" and "schoolgirls," kept their intelligence and insights under wraps (or hoods), revealing their talent to me only in an essay or a private conversation. Veronica begged me not to use her brilliant rebuttal of Dennis Kearney's speech as an example in class. Donald got upset that I had called his parents to commend his poetry because his brother overheard and told everyone at school how "sensitive" he is. The conversations go something like this:

Ms. Braimah: Veronica, can we talk after class?

Veronica: Why? I didn't do nothin'!

Ms. B: No, it's nothing bad. It will only take a minute.

V: 'K.

(after class)

Ms. B: Veronica, I was really impressed with your Dennis Kearney paper. You really understood the rhetoric he was using and did a good job refuting his arguments with evidence. I gave you an A-minus.

V: Cool. That's my best grade in your class.

Ms. B: If you want a solid A, you could do a rewrite. It's just a few grammatical and syntactical errors.

V: Naw. A-minus is cool.

Ms. B: OK. So would you mind if I shared it with the class as an example of a strong use of rhetoric?

V: No, Ms. Braimah! It's too embarrassing!

Ms. B: I'd take your name off the paper.

V: They would know anyway.

Ms. B: Please consider it. It would really help others learn what good writing looks like.

V: Uh-uh. Just use Justin's. People know he's smart anyway.

Ms. B: There's no shame in doing good work, Veronica.

(Veronica looks down at her feet in silence.)

Ms. B: OK. Well, at least think about it. I'll ask again tomorrow.

If I can't even get students to share work anonymously, how can I expect them to publicly engage in a debate on immigration reform? I thought my job was to teach standards, but getting students to exhibit higher-order thinking required so much more: I had to make them feel safe enough in my class to display some thoughtfulness.

They also needed to learn that there are no shortcuts to brilliance. Sean, having worked so hard on his comparative analysis of Malcolm X and Frederick Douglass, was devastated to receive a D on his first draft. He threatened to give up, believing that his effort had gone unrewarded. "I worked so hard on this, Ms. Braimah! How could it be a D?" "Sean," I replied, "don't think of it as a D. Think of it as 'not an A, *yet*.' Even the best writers can produce weak first drafts. Writing takes a lot of work and reworking to be really good." We then had a couple of writing conferences where we examined the grading rubric and identified specific areas to improve. I showed how something as simple as strengthening his thesis statement would yield 15 extra points on the rubric. After we sat together and worked on a good thesis statement, he grudgingly reworked his essay, bringing it up to a B+. His final thesis statement was so good that I used it as an example in the class (with his name removed, of course).

On the next assignment he handed me his paper with a wink and said, "Ms. Braimah, it's a'ight, but it's not an A . . . yet." Sean had learned that writing is a process. Am I overreaching to hope that he may also come to see that getting it right in life is a process? That failure is not really failure, it's just not success . . . yet?

Again, it's the small victories. My students may not all become the great thinkers of their generation, but I like to believe that when they sit at the table of a college seminar, or at the dinner table with friends and family, they will spontaneously challenge someone's thinking and be a force to reckon with. I am also so bold as to think that when that does happen, my class will have had something to do with it.

In the meantime, I've got standards to meet and tests to prepare for. I can't waste time pondering such frivolity as intellectual inspiration and awakening. And anyway, Whitman's captain may have been a hero, he may have been exalted, but in the final verse he is "Fallen cold and dead." Robin Williams's John Keating, despite his students' adulation, was fired. Me, I still have a job, and some good memories of small victories, minor insights, and major academic growth for my students.

THE NOUN LESSON

Tisha Riccio

I AM ONE OF those unusual individuals who are not settled in one profession. I am a teacher, a florist, and a restaurateur. I love each one of my professions for very different reasons. When I am asked, "Why teach, when the other two jobs just seem like so much fun?" I think of spectacular moments like this one:

Back in my early days of teaching, I taught in a resource position at a parochial school for first, second, and third graders. My classroom was a makeshift space that I made work by scouring the entire school for unused furniture, books, and manipulatives (learning materials). My room had no walls; I shared a large open space with another bigmouthed Italian on the other side of the room teaching middle graders algebra.

My first-grade partner teacher was magnificent. She entrusted her little darlings to me for the first two hours of her day with the grace and the confidence I needed in this somewhat challenging environment. I had a heterogeneous group of 18 bright-eyed first learners that taught me the lessons of my life.

As teachers, we know that review is the key to long-term learning. I had been working on the subject of nouns. We all know the generic definition of nouns: a noun is a person, place, or thing. Right? Well, not this particular day. In reviewing nouns, I chose a very eager participant, Dominique, to assist me in the process. Dominique enthusiastically raised her hand with an "Ooh, ooh, I know, Ms. Riccio. Pick me!" How could I resist the ponytailed little dear? Her answer, after holding her breath with the all-knowing excitement: "A noun is when a person plays with a thing." So proud! How could I burst that response? My colleague saw my expression from her side of our room. She shared in my shock/joy in this precious child's answer. "From the mouths of babes" was her take on the situation. It took all my self-control not to laugh but to thank Dominique for her help and move on.

I now teach freshman English in a predominantly Hispanic school. I always tell my Dominique story whenever the subject of nouns comes up. They get the preciousness of the child in that story. They get that answer. It makes them smile, just as it continues to make me smile.

And Dominique? She is now a lovely young lady attending our local parochial high school.

TRICKERY IN HISTORY

Tiffany Grizzle

ANOTHER YEAR MEANT another round of U.S. history for my fifth-grade students. It was my mission to make each time period interesting and relevant to the lives of 11-year-olds living in the age of Xbox. It was no small task, as the textbook's opening act was the migration across the land bridge between Russia, the Soviet Union, the former Soviet Union—you get my drift—and Alaska; and we were expected to cram all the historical information between that time and the 1970s into those eager little minds in the span of a single school year. I was usually lucky to make it to World War II without my classroom erupting into World War III.

Somewhere between *Sesame Street* and higher

education, a loathing of all things historical seems to infect the minds of students. There is an irrational fear that "social studies" translates to memorizing the Preamble or spouting out the year of every major war between 1756 and 1996. I was given the task of motivating my students to do more than whine and cringe when I uttered the taboo sentence "Take out your social studies books and turn to page . . ." (You can almost hear the collective groan, can't you?)

One of the most painful units seemed to be "the New World," learning all about the trials and tribulations of European immigrants in what is now the United States of America.

"This is the story of the birth of our nation!"

"Without these people's sacrifices, we wouldn't be here!"

"What a great adventure this was!"

No matter what spin I put on it, I was met mostly with eye rolls, stifled yawns, and questions about why all the pictures were drawings at the beginning of the history book and photos at the end. Ah, fifth graders!

Never one to be a huge proponent of worksheets, I was always looking for a way to give my kids a more hands-on learning experience. There was nothing worse than trudging, uphill, barefoot in the snow, through a rather dry textbook that was, quite frankly, not written with most fifth-grade readers in mind. I wasn't looking for students to just read and regurgitate information back onto a test only to forget that same information the minute they left the classroom.

But this year would be different! This year I would try something new! Something exciting! Something that was way more work for me, but I had every hope that it would be worth it. For all three sections of my fifth-grade history classes, I was going to immerse my students in an interactive game of discovery. I would have full-color charts and artwork, maps, and games. It wasn't exactly laser-tag exciting, but I did my best to appeal to their competitive nature. I had every hope that I could bridge the gap between monotonous textbook garble and meaningful connections to history.

Much like the Oregon Trail games I remembered from elementary school, this game simulated groups of immigrants trying to establish a colony in the New World. Students were assigned to teams, randomly, and then had to choose a leader, decide on supplies and routes, and devise a survival plan, without killing each other first! Upon hearing that a game was involved, a vast majority of my classes thought it was a free pass to play instead of learn for three weeks. Once they saw how much critical thinking, cooperation, and strategy went into every step, however, they realized they were in for more than just a few rounds of Chutes and Ladders.

Each class would begin with a dealing of game cards to each team, or colony. Colonies met with tragedy at sea, hailstorms that destroyed newly planted crops, plagues that wiped out half their colony's population; with each card dealt, the students were whipped into a frenzy of deciding what to do next in order to get one step closer to winning the game. I would walk around the room, listening to conversations about their budget to buy supplies, which natives to trade with, which natives they might have to fight with over land, and marveled at their ability to forget whether they really got along with each other outside the classroom as they huddled over their maps and supply lists, plotting and scheming.

There were discussions of why people would risk so much and live such a hard life in a new and strange world. It was difficult for these kids to imagine being so discriminated against that sailing for months on the ocean, only to arrive in an unknown land where they would have to start over from scratch, was, for some, their only hope. Of course, the boys loved the stories of battles between the Native Americans and the settlers, while many girls were horrified at the numbers of men, women, and children who succumbed to hideous illnesses. I, with stealthlike precision, managed to work in content from the history books so the game they were playing took on meaning to them by painting a picture of what life was like for those trying to colonize the eastern seaboard.

As the game went on, I began to witness a strange phenomenon. My students were discussing history outside the confines of my classroom. They were asking me questions at recess; they were sitting with their "colonies" at lunch to figure out what to do the next day. I had managed to help them break through some kind of invisible barrier and actually had a hand in piquing their interest to the point of the game becoming water cooler talk—or, in their case, juice box talk!

I realized that, as much credit as I gave my students, they deserved even more for sinking their teeth into this. But were they getting anything out of it other than the thrill of competition?

Days went by, and the card dealings became more and more exciting. Cheers would erupt from colonies with good fortune; heads would sink into the hands of those who met with catastrophe. As we charted each colony's progress on large maps on the classroom wall, the students began to realize the end was in sight, and the day came when we declared a winner and our game came to an end. The next day each class had a discussion about what had transpired—how hard the colonies had to work, how much luck factored into prosperity, how each decision they made affected the entire population—and I started to see that they had gotten a glimpse of what it must have been like for the early settlers of this nation.

The final period of the day, the third round-table discussion I had been part of, proved to be the most interesting. I thought I had heard everything by that point, only to be enlightened by a usually very quiet student. As class drew to a close and we were reviewing all the points made in class that day, this student shared an epiphany. "Wait a minute. This whole time we have been arguing about what to buy and what to plant, where to settle, and all the other stuff. That's what the settlers had to do, but they were actually there, and if they made bad decisions, the colony might not make it, like that Roanoke colony?" Hallucination or not, I swear I saw the lightbulb over his head.

"Exactly," I replied. "It must have been hard to live that life, don't you think?"

"Yeah, I thought it was hard to be a colony with just the five kids in my group, but it would've been way harder with hundreds of people, trying to survive for real. They must've wanted to start a new life more than anything else to put up with that."

"I think that's an excellent point you've just made."

"Wow, Mrs. Grizzle, it was really sneaky of you to put learning about all that stuff into one game. I didn't even know it had all gotten in my head until now!"

Mission accomplished.

I'm Good
at This Stuff!

Vicki Lautsch

DURING THE SUMMER after my first year of teaching, I convinced my administration to have an advanced sixth-grade math class that I could teach, to prepare a whole group of students to take algebra as seventh graders. I was excited to finally have an advanced class, and I was full of ideas on how to challenge the kiddos. Fast-forward to the first day of school, when the kids are introducing themselves to each other in this pre-algebra class. I asked them all who their previous teachers were, and a grinning Carlos raised his hand and asked, "Well, can't I say that you were, since I was in your room every day for lunch detention last year?"

Ah, Carlos. Yes, I remember your pitiful face, forced to be in my classroom for lunch detention almost every day of your fifth-grade year. Apparently I was scary enough that all the fifth graders were petrified of getting detention for fear of having to sit through my math class, where I frequently made them come to the board, do sixth-grade math work, and justify their answers. But not Carlos. He kept coming back.

Carlos had a rude awakening when he came into pre-algebra. We were a full house, 29 students, a good majority of them gifted and reading above grade level. One student, Samantha, who had a reputation for being more brilliant than her older sister (which to me seemed impossible because her sister finished her year by teaching herself how to sequence multiplying two-term polynomials using algebra tiles), blew us all away with her uncanny ability to absorb information. Alex, just as fantastic, had such a way with words that he could take a convoluted problem and use the most precise language to answer it with one sentence. Sabrina and Janine could solve any problem when they worked together . . . and never complained about it. Julian had a way of being able to ask one question and immediately understand the underlying concept behind the math; and Santos was the student who, when asked a question about kings doing work, would reply, "Why would kings ever work? The slaves would do the jobs for them." These shining stars made pre-algebra 80 minutes of pure discovery and a huge mathematical journey. They came into class wanting to be challenged and working at a pace that rivaled advanced high-school classes. And then there was Carlos.

Carlos described himself as "the last person to get placed in the class." If you asked him, he would frequently say that he didn't belong. He was a bright student and in any other classroom would be a go-to genius, but here there were too many main characters in the story. He had to play a supporting role, and his confidence level wavered. He was a student who, if in a wheelbarrow at the top of a hill, could lean all his body weight toward the front of the barrow but *never* go down the hill without a push. A swift push. A hard push. Perhaps an earthquake-sized push.

I considered him my personal challenge. None of my other students needed a push. When I told them that they got a 95 on a test, they came back with, "Well, can I retake it to get a hundred?" I would lead them through discoveries, and 20 minutes in, they would claim, "We got this, Lautsch. Shut up." Carlos, on the other hand, needed a fire lit under his tail.

The problem is that success breeds confidence, which breeds success, and the circle goes around. Carlos was trying to be successful, but he was just one step behind the rest of the class. Frequently he would leave class with his head hanging, claiming, "I'm too stupid to be in here. I never get it." It pained me to see him like that.

I tried everything. We studied after school. (That didn't work.) He sat in the front, very close to me. We used manipulatives (and when you're teaching algebra, dusting off those algebra blocks takes some work). He sat by his buddies. He sat by Samantha. He sat by Alex. We did group work. We did remedial work. I got the middle-school math teacher to come in and try to teach Carlos another way. But he still struggled. It was like we were all cruising down Highway 1 in our motorcycles, and Carlos was sprinting behind in a leather jacket. He just couldn't catch up.

I was so distraught that I brought in my master's professor. (I know, the woman who grades me! She decides whether I pass or fail, and I had just confessed that I cannot teach a child!) She watched and told me I was too hard on him. So I backed off, gave him his space. Perhaps I was trying to "give him space to grow" or something equally holistic. That didn't work either.

So let's fast-forward to an important part of the year. We are all older and wiser—but mostly more hormonal. Something strange happens in the middle of sixth grade: the sweetness of fifth grade fades away, which is sad, but the mental acuity of the kids' little brains as they develop is fun to watch. They think differently—pose more complex questions, develop more cohesive arguments, and bask in the glory of conceptual learning. This is the time that I love to teach algebra—to move from the concrete to the abstract and watch their minds work.

Also, by now the pressure of performing for the state has been reduced. The big "state test" has come and gone, and we can all dive into the fun stuff: the knowledge and skills the kiddos need to be successful in their advanced class next year. Here we are, solving complex algebraic equations. This is a major predictor of how a student will do in algebra the following year. Needless to say, I want to get this material solidly mastered before we move on.

I get an email from the professor I had called in, saying, "We need to videotape you as your last observation for your degree. This is your final show!" The date she names for her visit turns out to be the same day I'm teaching advanced equation-solving. So she comes in with her camera, we do our warm-up, I switch on the Smartboard with my interactive presentation, fully aligned to my objective, and—of course—the computer shorts out and the Smartboard breaks. *The woman is videotaping this.*

I'm visibly frazzled, trying to make up a lesson in my head (because I cannot even print the lesson with a dead computer) and we get out our whiteboards. The kids are eager, ready—but not Carlos. His head is low; he's showing fear, especially when I explain that this stuff is "very advanced" and "may be hard for some of you." The camera swoops to see his face, my frazzled face . . . Oh, I wish I could disappear right there.

The lesson begins. We're taking notes, working through steps, solving for variables together, and then,

I give them the first problem to try without me. Carlos's face has changed from fearful to determined. *I cannot believe I'm seeing this,* I think in my head. The class is eerily silent, working on their boards. They have to solve it on the whiteboard, and then flash it to me. (Obviously, with my being unprepared, I don't actually know the answers to the questions that I give because I have to solve them as I'm making them up. You try making up algebraic equations that use the distributive property and negative integers on the fly . . .) I'm solving the equation, I look up, and Carlos's board is the first one in the air. He has a huge grin on his face. *Oh crap,* I think. I haven't seen this face in math class before.

"Wait, Carlos, I don't have the answer yet . . . " And I double-check my work. I smile, point at his board, give him the thumbs-up, and say, "Yup." He turns his board around, looks at it, turns it back, and says, "What about me?"

"Carlos, I said yes."

"Yes what?"

"Yes, it's right."

His face lights up brighter than glitter eye shadow on a teenybopper. I have never seen a smile that wide. "I got it? Right? The first time?" I walk over to him and whisper, "Yes, you did."

I give them about five more problems to solve. Carlos is first on every one, always correct, his eyes brighter and brighter every time. He keeps leaning over to his tablemates, offering suggestions on how to solve these equations. "Can't you see it?" he asks them. I'm almost in tears, because it is the first time I've ever seen him this happy in math class. My professor never takes the camera off this kid and our interactions. The bell rings, and as everyone else is leaving the room, Carlos cleans up slowly and says, "I finally get it." I answer, "Yes, you finally do." A million thoughts rush through my head as students are cleaning their desks and heading out of the room. He finally got it! He just needed a little more time than everyone else. It must have been my backing off, letting him work at his own pace. Not every child is ready to learn these abstract concepts at the same pace at the same time in their lives. Wouldn't it have been nice if someone had told me that *before* I started teaching? He wasn't ready to go this fast with material in the beginning of the year. He's older now, more mature. I had to wait until *he* was ready to master these concepts.

He walks out of the room, stops, and says, "What's math going to be like next year?" I say, "A lot more of stuff like this."

His reply has stuck with me forever: "Good. I'm good at this stuff."

■

THE ART OF
THE RELATIONSHIP
IN TEACHING

THE DAY AUSTIN FOUND
HIS INSIDE VOICE

"Miss D"

AUSTIN WOULD BECOME the most exhausting student I have ever met in my life—and one who changed my view of education entirely.

I worked for three years in a K–1 classroom for children who receive special education services. The first year I was the paraprofessional in the room, and the following years I was the lead teacher. All my students were high-functioning, and the majority of the accommodations they needed involved helping them with attention, social skills, and dealing with emotions. Austin came to my classroom in November the first year I worked at this school. We had gotten a new student a month earlier, and I had been stressed that he was going to disrupt the positive flow we had going with our kids. Then he turned out to be one of our best-behaved kids! So this time, I was *sure* we'd be fine.

For the first few months we had Austin, he would scream at the top of his lungs for hours on end until he lost his voice. He would scream over nothing at all or over very little things. Rarely could he even identify what was bothering him. The only thing that would keep him calm was playing on the computer, but playing all day on the computer is hardly an education. Despite his screaming, we had high expectations for Austin. Austin would scream at other children who tried to play with him. He threw furniture. He said "That's crap!" about everything.

On the third day of having Austin in our classroom, I cried during the middle of lunch. He was taking all my energy, and nothing I did seemed to have any impact. I couldn't even have a conversation with the kid about anything. He didn't like any food. He didn't like any colors. He didn't like any toys. No TV shows. No people. No songs. Nothing. There was nothing the kid liked. Before we got Austin, our class was the best behaved in the school. Austin wound our other kids up, just by how loud he could be.

One day Austin walked around the room and sat at the computer chanting "No more demons in my house" for over 20 minutes straight. I couldn't get him to stop, and it was scaring the other kids. I took Austin for a walk to give my teaching partner and the other kids a break. During that walk, Austin told me he wasn't good at anything and he was a bad person. I asked him why he thought that, and he said it was because he did bad things. I got down to Austin's eye level and told him people make mistakes. Kids have trouble knowing what to do sometimes. Someone can make big mistakes in the outside world, but still be very good on the inside. He told me he didn't know if he believed me.

I told Austin every day that he was my friend or that I cared about him. I never let him leave without making sure I'd told him, because I didn't know if anyone else in his life told him those things.

Slowly, Austin began to respond to me. I could get him to tell me about his cats. I could get him to complete half his work. When the school psychologist had to do Austin's IQ testing, he flat-out refused to cooperate. The behavior specialist couldn't get him to do it. The principal couldn't get him to do it. I walked in and within three minutes he began cooperating.

Austin had a coping mechanism that involved hoarding things and keeping them in his pocket. It was usually coins or coupons that he thought would get him free food. He was very concerned about being poor. However, the items in his pocket were often distracting to him and others. I made a rule; he could keep the items as long as they stayed in his pocket. If I saw them, they were mine until the end of the day.

This rule often resulted in *major* meltdowns. But now we were at the point where he just had silent tears streaming down his face (which was actually harder on me than the screaming). One day I told Austin that if he brought coins the next day, I would keep the coins for a whole week. He was better off just not bringing them. Sure enough, no coins the next day. But he did have other things in his pocket. The day after that, he had a fake coin in his pocket. He took it out during gym class and I told him if I saw it again I was going to take it away. He took it out an hour later, and I just stuck out my hand. He put it in my palm, and I asked what else he had in there. He pulled out a turtle. What else? A robot. What else? A Spider-Man glove. The kid pulled out 12 things! I felt like he was a clown car. He had tears streaming down his face. I really thought the objects were a comfort thing for him. I told him I would put them in a bag and put them on the windowsill by his desk, but if he touched them, I would have to put them in his mailbox. "Yes, ma'am." And he didn't touch them. The following week he came up to me at ten o'clock. "Miss D!"

"Yes, Austin?"

"I don't have anything in my pockets!"

First time all year! I was so proud! This was huge.

Austin gradually began to grow academically and socially. He started to have conversations with the other kids. He participated in class discussions. But with summer drawing near, I was worried that a lot of the progress we had made would be lost in the upcoming months. Austin was still convinced that he was a bad person; he thought the world would be better off if he had never been born. I had many talks with him about how important he was and all the good things he did. It never seemed like he believed me. We had other staff members involved and had been working with his mom to get him the support he needed. However, only with me would he discuss how he felt and why he was angry at times. I was thrilled to learn that I would be the lead teacher the following school year and that Austin would be in my class as a first grader.

We were only two weeks into the new school year when Austin was truly tested. He was angry because he had made a mistake on a worksheet. He chose to walk away from his desk in order to give himself some time to cool down. Upon leaving his chair, he accidentally knocked it to the floor. One of my other students promptly shouted out, "*Ooh,* Austin is *baaaad!*" I braced myself for an explosion. I put myself in between the two children, and before I could say anything to either child, Austin stunned us all.

In the calmest voice I have ever heard a child use when angry, Austin told the other child, "I am not bad. You don't know me. You don't know I'm good. You don't know I'm bad. I knocked over a chair. I shoulda been more careful, but I was trying my best. Just because someone makes a mistake or says something mean does not make them bad on the inside. They are probably very good on the inside. So even though I knocked down a chair and you said something mean, we're both probably good."

The rest of the year wasn't a breeze, but everyone in the class knew that everyone was good on the inside from that moment on. It allowed us all to forgive each other's mistakes and to cheer each other on.

FROM TENNESSEE, HERE TO MODEL

Sheri A. Castro-Atwater, PhD

I T WAS WINTER 2001, midway through my year as a
school psychologist intern, when it hit me: I am in the
right profession. Never before had I observed so many
acts of kindness from teachers reaching out to children
who needed a caring hand.

I loved the new responsibilities of my position and
the enjoyment I received from meeting and consulting
with teachers in my new elementary-school assignment. One of these teachers, Mrs. Knopff, asked me
to observe her fifth-grade classroom. Her class was a
haven, a cool, sunny room with an outdoor balcony
overlooking Alameda, California. I sensed that the

children knew they were in a special place too. The soft murmuring classroom "buzz," generally mellow and happy, echoed out into the hallway. Although this was considered a "troubled" Title 1 school, the atmosphere felt safe and caring. By this point in my training, I had been in enough schools to know this atmosphere could not be taken for granted; it was the kind of culture that teachers worked hard to create, developing camaraderie among themselves that spilled out into the hallways and into the school. From the students I had worked with, I knew this was in stark contrast to the chaos that many of them experienced at home.

I was there on a day when a new African American student was coming to the class, from Memphis, Tennessee. Mrs. Knopff had asked me to observe the dynamics of the classroom to see if I could help create a friendly environment for the new girl. I believed I was really here to see if I could entice some of the fifth-grade girl cliques to learn about and accept this new student. Female cliques in Mrs. Knopff's class had been a contentious issue since the start of the year (backstabbing, ignoring, switching allegiances, and instant making up had become increasingly common), and the weekly girls' group I was running always threatened to become the center stage where these upsets were aired.

The new girl, Henrietta Long, was expected to arrive midday; she was being dropped off at the school by her parents. She walked in midway through math.

Immediately I sensed she felt shy and awkward, embarrassed to have stopped the class and to feel 22 pairs of eyes turn toward her. She looked different from the other children too. Though they were a variety of ethnicities and cultures, all the other girls in the class had jeans, backpacks, and sneakers (the standard "uniform" of California schools). Henrietta carried a lunch pail, had her hair in two braids with ribbon, and wore an orange gingham dress, with black Mary Janes on her feet. A beautiful and foreign-looking girl to the class; they were sizing her up. A couple of giggles erupted from the two female-clique leaders; knowing, critical glances flew like electrical pulses quickly across the room. *This girl is odd,* they said silently to each other. *She's not making it into* our *group.*

Mrs. Knopff, in her quick and perceptive way, must have caught all of this. To my amazement, she stopped the class. "Henrietta, there you are! Welcome! I am so glad you're here. We're just learning how to do these division problems, the ones you and I discussed together yesterday. I was going to ask one person from each group to share their secret shortcut with us. I'm so glad you dressed up just as I suggested, since we're . . . doing the pictures today too."

The class was confused. Mrs. Knopff quickly grabbed a disposable camera from her desk and headed toward the back of the class.

"Could you go up to the front, Henrietta? Put your

things down in that desk over there"—she pointed to a seat near Alicia, clique leader number one—"and go up and grab some chalk. Would you mind pointing to the answer to the problem on the left?" Mrs. Knopff began clicking away. "Great, great," she murmured, "now point to how we do the shortcut, remember? Good, good . . . This will be perfect for the district magazine. Now turn toward the left, a bigger smile . . ."

In a matter of seconds, Henrietta's demeanor switched from shy and awkward to engaged, with that innocent air that children have when they sense they are doing something serious and important. More impressively, I could see that in the other children's minds, Henrietta went from an overdressed, foreign newcomer to a budding model (a profession I knew from my girls' group many of them aspired to).

Hands shot up. "Can I be next, Mrs. Knopff?" "I want to go next!" Mrs. Knopff glanced lovingly but with a critical eye at the other hopeful models. "Hm . . . Shirlene, you'd be a great model, but you're wearing those jeans with a hole; maybe next time when you know you're modeling and can bring something a bit more professional-looking. I'll let you know."

Several years later I still remember that moment, how the critical classroom tone shifted so quickly to one of openness. I didn't witness an amazing cure-all to guarantee universal acceptance or even an ingenious remark that made everything bode well for Henrietta. It was just

Mrs. Knopff being Mrs. Knopff, an adept teacher as sensitive to the social and emotional needs of her preadolescent students as she was to their academic ones.

I was, and continue to be, inspired.

⊞

HOW THE SPERM GETS TO THE EGG

Lin Cerles, PhD

A s a teacher, I find I often focus on talkative children who ask lots of questions. I am less likely to notice the quiet, shy child who complies with the rules and rarely raises her hand.

Last year I had a student, Sonja, who excelled academically but never said a word in class. She was painfully shy and self-conscious, not wanting to be wrong, or even to be seen. As an adult educator I look back and wish that teachers had been more demanding of my own class participation and that they had set up a classroom environment that felt safe—where one wouldn't feel embarrassed for asking a silly question or responding to a question wrongly. It's easy to find a teachable moment for a child who is inquisitive or active or outspoken. It's quite another to find a way to reach the shy children, who rarely raise their hands, hate to be noticed, and often fail to give a clue as to what's confusing or unclear. Often the teachable moments for these children occur only when the child has been brave enough to participate or to answer a question.

My own most memorable moment as a student occurred in sixth grade, when I raised my hand (probably for the first time that year) to ask the teacher how the sperm in the man gets to the egg in the female. We had just heard the news about menstrual periods and pregnancy, but no one explicitly said how the sperm and the egg got together. Unbelievably, at age 12, I honestly had no idea. After I asked the question, the class all turned to look at me with shock on their faces. The teacher muttered something about "let's talk about it later," folded up his notebook, and ended the lesson. It gradually dawned on me that the question had been an inappropriate one, but I had no idea why. One friend said to me, "You *really* don't know?" Well, I ran home and pulled down from my parent's bookshelf a book called *The Naked Ape* and read about how the sperm gets to the egg. Of course, I was mortified to think that I had shown my ignorance about sex to my whole sixth-grade class. I don't believe I raised my hand again that year or even the next. To this day, I still need to feel very comfortable in a group before I ask a question or offer a comment.

As a teacher I see that finding teachable moments for shy children like myself and Sonja requires a great deal of thought and planning. These children are difficult to notice when we are faced with 30 children, probably half of whom are clamoring for our attention. It's very easy to overlook the shy child. Shy children often fear their teachers. Shy children do not necessarily have emotional disorders or learning disabilities. Rather, they perceive a vague threat, which causes discomfort, usually a threat of social embarrassment. In general, they need to be integrated into the classroom at a slower pace.

Last year I consciously created some strategies to deal with Sonja, who reminded me of myself. I gave her time to warm up to changes in seating or unusual transitions. I communicated with her parents, who had not been aware that their daughter was withdrawn at school. I made sure that the more aggressive children in the class, who occasionally bullied her verbally, were monitored. I let her role-play with other children. I divided the class into groups, putting her with other quiet children rather than with extremely confident and gregarious children. I encouraged her conversational skill by asking her open-ended questions, which encouraged her to speak up without fear of giving a wrong answer. I integrated social skills into the curriculum. Sonja, an excellent reader, was able to understand how characters in a story became friends. As she gained confidence, I placed her in cooperative learning groups with other children who had various levels of social skills. She was ready to follow the lead of her more outgoing peers.

Most importantly, I felt a real breakthrough with Sonja when I let her know about my own shyness as a child and my continuing struggle with speaking up in groups. I made an informal agreement with her that I would sometimes call on her when I knew she knew the answer, and I reassured her that I wished my teachers had done that more with me when I was a student. We know as educators that teachers who ask simple yes-or-no questions receive brief responses from their students, but those who volunteer personal information or make insightful comments while asking few direct questions are rewarded with more in-depth responses and participation.

Next time one of my students asks a "How does the sperm get to the egg?" question, I'll be sure to answer with empathy and sensitivity, hoping it won't be the last time that student raises her (or his) hand in class that year.

I'M NOT DOIN' ANY WORK TODAY!

Randy Howe

I SEE THE WORLD through rose-colored glasses. One reason is that on many an occasion I have been in the right place at the right time. Good luck may be, as some say, the result of hard work, but most of the pivotal moments in my professional life have been pure serendipity. This was especially true in my first years of teaching. It was a random conversation with a professor that pushed me to pursue a master's in special education, and while earning that degree I lucked upon my first job. I was hired to be the academics instructor in a teen parenting program.

"These are young girls and you're a young man," the director warned during an interview, but I never had any of that kind of trouble with them. The hardest part was simply getting them to class on time. We had a nursery, so their babies came to school with them, and parting was such sweet sorrow. I was gung-ho about my lessons but understood that an extra minute of cuddling would trump slope-intercept form, the Founding Fathers, and *Lord of the Flies* every time. One young lady, though, seemed to have no trouble leaving her daughter behind. As a matter of fact, she usually came to class early.

"Mr. Howe!" I'd hear from the hallway, my lunch not yet finished. "I'm not doin' any work today!" Then she would enter the room.

"Hi, Joanna. How's it going?"

"Good!" she'd say, and with the weight of her responsibilities, thump down into a seat. I'd requested tables with chairs, rather than the typical desk-chair attachments, because many of the girls could not fit comfortably. Some returned to their fighting weight moments after passing the placenta, while others kept the pounds on. Joanna had a lot of baggage, both physically and emotionally, and somewhere along the line she'd decided to compensate for this by dominating the room. Even questions came with an exclamation point attached.

"What we learnin' today?!"

I knew what I was teaching—a lesson on the school shooting at Columbine High School and school safety plans—but I wasn't sure how she planned on "learnin'" without "doin'."

"Current events. I want to discuss lockdowns and—"

"Hmph!"

I'd asked her about the refusal to do work before, but that tree had yet to bear fruit. I never asked about her leaving Asia, her daughter, earlier than necessary. I'd been advised to avoid questions that might sound judgmental.

"Columbine's got nothin' to do with me!"

I switched gears, fending off the instinct to win both battle and war. "Did you know that Columbine is actually the name of a flower? It's—"

"No!"

I shut down my computer and the bell rang. Joanna sat with arms crossed, a show of how little faith she had in the day's plans.

With copies of a *USA Today* article ready to go, I wanted to discuss what had happened at Columbine, but more importantly, how we could make sure that nothing like that ever happened here. The most successful lessons were those that tapped into the girls' role as mothers. I hoped that the maternal instinct would help us to avoid an afternoon of simple name-calling—"maniacs" or "murderers"—and knee-jerk cries for capital punishment. The objective was to brainstorm a plan that I could share with fellow members of the School Emergency Team. I knew that the girls might have some pretty good ideas, given that the motivation was their safety. Theirs and their children's. I wondered if Joanna would be so inclined. Some teen mothers, I'd been told, actually resent their children.

As the rest of the girls filed in, some of them noticeably ignoring the mother who'd left her baby before the bell, I counted heads. Nine present, three absent or at least running late after a tearful goodbye. I always designed a lengthy introduction to the afternoon's lesson to accommodate these latecomers.

"Those were some crazy brothers," Jillian said, after I let them know what we'd be doing.

"Do you mean 'brothers' as in siblings?" I asked, keeping a hopeful eye on the door. "Or as in friends?"

"Whatever. All I know is they was crazy to kill themselves like that."

"And crazy to kill everyone else!" Joanna added. She wasn't fond of paper-and-pencil tasks but did participate in class. Most of Joanna's grades I had in my book were from oral assessments.

"How do you define 'crazy'?" I asked, giving the stragglers one more minute and regretting that they would miss this important point. I knew a little bit about postpartum depression and understood that a discussion on mental illness was relevant for all teens. Melanie, the program's social worker, had been an invaluable resource for me in that regard.

The article for our lesson was about Dave Sanders, one of the teachers killed at Columbine. I didn't know it yet, but one year later a student who had witnessed

Sanders' death would take his own life. A mother of a girl who was wounded that day would do the same. Perhaps we would discuss the comparisons between post-traumatic stress disorder and postpartum depression. I also had in mind the statistics about abuse in girls who grow up to be teen mothers. Add in the fact that three-quarters of my students were diagnosed with a disability, and the potential for emotional problems increased exponentially.

Serious business, for sure, but all my friends got a kick out of this little one-room schoolhouse of mine. I was a 28-year-old man surrounded by teenage girls who'd had sex. The jokes almost wrote themselves, from *Charlie's Angels* references on down, but I could tell that people were legitimately interested in what I did and who I worked with. I found myself answering a lot of questions at parties and not minding it one bit. Serendipity had taken me down an unexpected path and I could talk about my teaching, and my students, all night long.

One thing I liked to tell people was that I learned as much from the girls as they did from me. Laughter would follow as I described learning how to wipe thoroughly during a diaper change, and then I would have some heartfelt talk about how complicated their lives were, how hard I worked to understand them. Then I'd follow up with something to lift the mood of the party back to where it belonged.

After one visit from Planned Parenthood, the girls covered my car with condoms. What sounded funny on a Saturday night was, in fact, an aggressive move that crossed some lines. I addressed it with all the girls and then let Melanie, the social worker, deal with them individually. Another time, a ringleader of a girl named Angel ambushed me with a photo from the hospital, her naked legs spread wide and her newborn's head the only thing between me and indecency. Angel was an angry girl who needed to test the limits to know where she stood. In both cases, photo and car, I was left feeling inadequate as a teacher. And so I continued to look for ways to learn from them so that they could learn from me.

Tangential conversations were often useful, but as expected, the topic of Columbine was engaging enough to keep them on track. Only one girl missed out, the two other tardies entering the room before I had to report them to the office. I was relieved to walk by and not smell cigarettes. They were done saying goodbye to their babies and we were ready to contemplate "crazy."

Maria defined it as the inability "to think clear." Echoing something she must have heard elsewhere, Kayla said it was "doing the same thing, again and again and again, but thinkin' that things'll turn out different." Bonita told us she thought that crazy was "bad wiring in the brain." When Joanna questioned that answer, I gave a brief description of frontal lobe research on people with violent histories and offered extra credit for more information as I passed out copies of the article.

After reading about Sanders, I drew a line down the

middle of the chalkboard. At the top of the left half, I wrote, "What happened?" I neglected to give a title to the right half, hoping that the mystery would help hold their attention.

"Twelve people got shot!" Joanna said, without raising her hand.

"Twelve people died," I wrote, then said, "More than twelve were shot."

"Whatever!" Joanna announced, trying to show how little she cared about being wrong but accomplishing the exact opposite.

Other girls added facts, but I was thinking about Joanna. She certainly had layers of armor, but how many layers I couldn't yet tell. As I wrote the names "Dylan Klebold" and "Eric Harris" on the board, I was thinking, *"But I'm gay now."* It surprised me, thinking of a boy I'd never met, the boy who had impregnated Joanna, rather than the two Colorado boys who had welcomed us all to the era of zero tolerance. It also surprised me because I think I understood that boy's motivations just as I understood Dylan and Eric's.

In Joanna's case, he didn't want to be a father. She was a student at a residential facility when she entered the gymnasium with him, the boy whose name she refused to say, even to Melanie. They had sex there and two months later, she learned she was pregnant. When Joanna told "Asia's father," he didn't miss a beat, replying, "But I'm gay now." In one fell swoop, he had relinquished all responsibility for the baby and for maintaining a relationship with the baby's mother. Whether it was the confidence of his words or the fact that Joanna felt she had no recourse, the boy had achieved his goal. Just like Dylan and Eric.

Finished with that side of the brainstorming, I added "Prevent from happening again" to the right side of the chalkboard. Before I could finish reminding them that there were no wrong answers when brainstorming, Joanna was speaking.

"I got one. Get people to quit lying to other people and maybe lie to the liars instead." The class turned toward Joanna's spot in the back, all except Angel, who chewed her gum in protest. "Let's make the fathers do all the work the mothers do and let's make the geeky computer kids play in a football game. Let's make those art kids clean up all the messy paint and stuff so they understand how hard it is for the janitor to clean up after them. Then let's make all the bullies stand with their hands behind their backs for dodgeball. The school should make the teachers take a test too. No, one of them surprise pop quizzes!" This got a cheer from the girls, even Angel. I considered adding it to the board, for humor's sake, but decided not to, opting instead to quit giving them pop quizzes.

I thought she was finished, but in an unusually quiet voice Joanna added, "They should make all the fat kids serve food in the cafeteria, 'cept they can't eat it." No mention of serving the lunch ladies, and I realized that, for once, Joanna was pointing the finger at herself. A lightbulb went on above my head, something not for this moment but for later. I had learned from a mentor that some teachable moments are, ironically enough, more effective with a planned delivery; "teachable moment" doesn't necessarily have to mean at that "moment."

Leaning back and recrossing her arms, Joanna let me know that she was done. I wrote on the board, "Teach empathy," and left it at that. Kayla recommended "locks on every door"—the School Emergency Team was already working on this, as many of our doors didn't even have locks—and Angel contributed "random sweeps with the wand." I asked if this would be better than metal detectors at the main entrance and they all agreed. Angel beamed. At day's end, I felt like a number of objectives had been achieved.

Driving home, my good mood led me back to Joanna's soliloquy. The usual exclamation points were missing, and she had revealed another complicated layer in an already complicated life. I found myself hoping that she would come to class early the next day. And of course she did.

"Mr. Howe!" I heard from outside my door and down the hall. "I'm not doin' any work today!"

Tuna sandwich already finished, computer shut down, I waited for Joanna to plop down and then moved to a seat at a neighboring table. With the sense that I was trying to control things, she immediately grew uncomfortable.

"You tryin' to talk to me about doin' homework?!"

"Nope, I just wanted to thank you for your comments yesterday."

She was stumped but managed to get her mouth moving as her brain caught up. "I didn't answer the questions at the end of that article, you know!" It dawned on me that Joanna was actually a lot like Angel.

"You basically led our discussion, Joanna. You were the brains behind our brainstorming!" Dramatic pause. "Have you thought about going to college?"

This was, I realized with great guilt, the first time in five years that I'd posed this question to one of my girls.

"Yes!"

"You have? That's great!" I was shocked not to have to convince her.

"Why you think I come to school every day? Why you think I come to class early?"

"I'm sorry. I didn't know. I think that would really be great for you and for Asia too."

The teachable moment I'd designed for her—had waited on, plotting and planning to get it just right; this college sell-job I was geared up for, saving the world one student at a time and relishing everyone's attention at the next party with another one of my stories—was, in truth, just another teachable moment for me. Serendipity.

I decided to go a step further, to roll the dice and

try to parlay this into something bigger for my college-bound kid.

"Would you be willing to attend our next School Emergency Team meeting? We could really use some student input."

"Nope!" she said, shaking her head for emphasis. "I got enough work to do as is!" Then the bell rang.

THE GIFT OF LITERACY

Erika Childs

I T DIDN'T TAKE long to realize that Shawnessa Cooper was going to need some extra attention. Maybe it was the fact that every time I turned around, I would nearly knock her over. She didn't leave my side her entire first day at our school. Or maybe it was the moment that I found that this fourth grader could barely read on an early first-grade level.

Shawnessa moved from Mississippi a few days after the school year began at our inner-city Las Vegas elementary school. With her bubbly personality, this charming African American girl began making friends instantly. She loved to talk and to keep up with the latest classroom drama, and would often be found in the middle of childhood love triangles. The boys were enamored, and the girls were often jealous of the attention. Shawnessa was also very talented at hiding the fact that she struggled in school. She would have her friends help her with assignments, reading passages for her, and she would find excuses not to answer questions in front of the class.

I quickly began working closely with Shawnessa during and after school. We went back to learning letter names and sounds, sight words, and decoding skills. She was determined to not let her new friends know she couldn't read, but she was just as determined to conquer her reading challenges when she was working with me. Despite her valiant efforts, the first couple of months felt like we were making very little progress. Each day the *b* and *d* were interchangeable. She seemed to assign long or short vowel sounds to words at random. We both were hitting a high frustration level.

I knew at this point that I would need to enlist some additional help in this battle. The work that she was putting in at school would have to be supported at home. The problem was that Shawnessa's mother did not want to work with me.

When I had first come to this school two years before, many parents made it very clear that they didn't want to have a white teacher in charge of their children's education. The cold reception I received from the parents was often passed on to their children. I had students tell me that they didn't like white people and that I should just go back where I came from. I learned that if I was to gain respect from the children, I would have to start with the parents. I began attending my students' football games, concerts, after-school activities, and neighborhood parties. I wanted the parents to know that I wasn't on some mission to save their children; my goal was to help each child recognize and reach his or her own potential. In order to successfully convey this message, I needed to show the students and the parents that I had a genuine interest in the community.

It has been very rewarding to see how these small efforts have begun to pay off. When I call home to discuss a concern about a student's academics or behavior, the parents are now willing to listen and support the suggestions on how we can work together to address the issue. The attitudes of the children have also changed. The days of pencils, paper, and chairs being thrown have nearly disappeared. Simply telling a student that I was disappointed in a poor choice has become more effective in changing behavior than many other consequences I have tried. The parents, students, and I have learned to respectfully work with each other toward the same goals.

Ms. Cooper and I initially had a pleasant relationship. We exchanged friendly greetings in the halls of the school. She would occasionally stop by the classroom to bring a forgotten homework assignment or library book. I would discuss the successes and concerns about Shawnessa's reading progress. I would let her know that Shawnessa had a gift for oral expression, but the middle of a math lesson is probably not the best time to have a heated discussion about the latest fourth-grade drama.

Everything changed during a meeting in the principal's office. One November day I was walking out to the playground to pick up my students from their PE class. As I turned the corner, I happened to see Shawnessa hit a boy in our class with all her might. Knowing the personalities of both students and having had to intervene in previous quarrels, I quickly started to piece together that Shawnessa had probably had enough of his constant teasing. After some investigation, it turned out that my hunch was correct. Both students were sent home for fighting and were to come back the next day with their parents to meet with the principal. I was called down to the office the next morning to join the meeting with Shawnessa, her mother, and the principal. Shawnessa seemed very nervous. Her loquaciousness was replaced with nods of the head and one-word answers. The more the situation was discussed, the more the tension in the room increased. Shawnessa wasn't speaking, her mother wasn't wanting to believe that her child would get in a fight, and I was having flashbacks to two years before, when I was the unwelcome stranger in the school. That office visit was the last time I heard Shawnessa's mother speak to me. I had lost the respect that I had worked so hard to earn because she was holding me responsible for her daughter's getting in trouble. The classroom visits stopped. Ms. Cooper would not even look at me if I saw her in the hallways.

Of course I was concerned that I had a parent upset with me (although it was definitely not the first time), but I was more anxious that Shawnessa was falling farther behind in school. It did not help the problem when I began to notice Shawnessa was following her mother's example. She was not showing the same eagerness to work with me as she had before the meeting. She would make comments to me about how I treated the white kids better than I treated her (even though there were no white kids in the class). The last thing she needed was another factor to hinder her progress. I felt discouraged, knowing that reinforcement of the reading skills at home was crucial and that finding this key piece seemed nearly impossible.

Parent-teacher conferences were scheduled a few weeks after the fight. I was relieved to see that Ms. Cooper agreed to come, but I was a little apprehensive about this meeting. I knew that this would be the perfect opportunity to introduce a plan on how to work with Shawnessa at home. I also knew that I would need some way to show her that I really did care about her and her family. Miraculously, the conversation went much better than expected. The discussion about academics went smoothly. Ms. Cooper was concerned to see that her daughter was so behind, but I could still sense a bit of hostility. Then the topic switched to things at home. I was trying desperately to find a way to connect with her so that we could work together. I asked her how the transition to a new city had been. She hesitantly began telling me about unexpected struggles she was facing. I learned that she hadn't been able to find a job despite the many applications she had submitted. She also mentioned how difficult it had been to explain to her three young children that Santa wouldn't be able to come to their house this year.

It wasn't until the last parent had left my classroom that I realized I had the perfect opportunity to help build a trusting relationship with the Cooper family. I grabbed my phone and called Ms. Cooper. She seemed a bit confused at first as to why I was calling. I explained that I would love to help her provide a Christmas for her family this year. She was hesitant at first, but I tried my best to explain that I just wanted to help make things easier for her during this stressful time. I think both of us were holding back tears as I hung up the phone with a list of clothing and shoe sizes for her kids. I knew that this small act was just the thing that would help Shawnessa receive at last her gift of literacy.

I could not believe how quickly things changed with Shawnessa after the winter break. During the first day back at school, Shawnessa and I sat at the back table struggling through some sight word flash cards. At one point I noticed she was wearing a sweater and a pair of shoes that I had dropped off at her house before the break, as well as a necklace from a little jewelry-making kit I had included with the packages of clothes. I complimented her on the necklace, and all of a sudden it seemed like the previous weeks of resistance toward me melted away. The girl who had worked so hard to distance herself was now talking a mile a minute about how her grandmother had helped her make the necklace and that she had a matching bracelet and earrings at home. She couldn't wait to show me the complete set the next day. It took a bit of convincing to get her to return to the work that we were doing, but as soon as she picked up those flash cards again, she began concentrating carefully on each word. It was exciting to see her confidence increase while she read a book that contained the words we had just practiced. She was remembering more words that day than she had in the past few weeks.

Every day after this small victory I would try to incorporate a personal connection into each lesson. She would write sentences using her siblings' names as the subject. I would find books and articles that matched her interests in fashion, animals, Hannah Montana, and Mississippi. I would always plan a couple of minutes at the beginning of each session to let her talk about whatever was on her mind. This seemed to help her focus better during the lesson, and it helped me find connections to use while we worked together.

Through the next month Shawnessa did start to make great gains. She began to become more fluent when she read. Her decoding was not the laborious task it had been initially. Her attitude toward me had improved as much as her reading ability. I knew that she was again following her mother's example. I also knew that her mother was following our plan at home. She was reading with her daughter each night and helping her with her homework. Ms. Cooper also began to stop by the classroom again. Sometimes the visits were to bring a forgotten item or check on Shawnessa's progress, but often it was just to give a quick hello.

One day in late January, Shawnessa raised her hand and asked me to help her with an unfamiliar word. It was exciting to watch her apply the decoding strategies we had been working on. Her face beamed when she realized that she had figured out the word *furious* all by herself. I took this opportunity to push her a bit further. "What does this word mean?" I asked. "Well," Shawnessa answered, "the boy in the story is always late to basketball practice. It says the coach felt 'furious.' So I think the clues are telling me that the word means 'mad.'" I am still not sure who felt more proud at that moment. The grin on Shawnessa's face told the whole story when I congratulated her on figuring that all out by herself. We both knew that the months of hard work, despite the setbacks, were paying off. The literacy lightbulb had been turned on.

A few days after this beautiful moment, Shawnessa announced that she would be moving back to Mississippi at the end of the week because her mom could get her old job back. A flood of emotions came over me. I was angry at the state of the economy. I was relieved to know that Ms. Cooper would be able to feed and clothe her children. I was sad to see such a great person leave my classroom. Most of all, I was disappointed that I would not get to watch Shawnessa continue to accomplish the goals that she had worked so hard to achieve.

Even though my time with the Cooper family was a short and tumultuous few months, I know that we all learned a lot from each other. On Shawnessa's last day of school, I got to tell her and her mother that she was reading 35 more words in a minute than she was when she first stepped into our classroom. Ms. Cooper then embraced me in one of the biggest hugs I have ever received. We both knew that this one hug meant so much more than "we will miss each other." It represented a closure to the racial tension and distrust and the beginning of one child's recognizing her potential to be successful at anything she worked hard to accomplish.

■

REACHING THE SPECIAL-NEEDS STUDENT

THE UNEXPECTED JOYS OF TEACHING

Jill Hare

I ARRIVED AT MY first teaching job bright and early on the first day of preplanning. The principal greeted me and said she'd lead me to my room. We took a flight of stairs to the basement. I could hear a basketball bouncing and reverberating off the gym floor. The sound got closer and louder, and then the principal stopped. She stood at the door of a small, dark room. It shared a wall and hallway with the school gymnasium and had no windows. As the principal turned to walk away, I flicked on the lights. Dirty tile floor and a teacher's desk with an enormous, outdated computer sitting on top. Sigh. I guessed teaching bright, happy music in this room to kindergartners through fifth graders would be challenging.

I tracked down a janitor, who helped me lug an old carpet out of storage for my room. With no desks or chairs to speak of, at least my students wouldn't have to sit on the floor collecting dust bunnies. I wanted my music class to be full of dancing and movement, so I looked on the positive side: there wouldn't be anything in the way! After exploring the previous music teacher's closet next to the boiler room, I found an entire almost brand-new set of Orff instruments—xylophones and metallophones. I lugged them back to my room and set up shop.

As I was planning my lessons, I got an email from my principal with the weekly schedule for my music classes. I glanced at Friday and did a double take: all of my classes on Friday were "doubles." Then I glanced around my room. Where was I going to put almost fifty students for each class on Friday?

My first four days of teaching flew by and then Friday came. As the day went on, my classes got bigger, literally. Starting with kindergarten, each hour brought older students with bigger bodies taking up more space in my tiny dungeon of a room. I felt pulled in all directions, but I was surviving and the kids were giddy with excitement at the activities I'd planned. When it came time for the second graders to enter my room, I stood at the door and watched them pile in. One boy was a bit taller than the rest. His teacher simply said, "That's Kirby. He's got Asperger's." She turned and left before I could ask her, "What's Asperger's?" Uh-oh. I racked my brain to remember Asperger's from my special-education classes in college. With no time to surf the Web or look at my college notes, I was facing on-the-job training.

Fifty pairs of eyes were staring up at me from the carpet. I began to sing a call-and-response song the kids could catch onto quickly. I scanned the crowd looking for Kirby. Among all the bright, silly faces singing back at me was his somber face. He was staring at my bulletin board. He wasn't singing. I tried to make eye contact with him, but had no luck.

We came to the movement part of my lesson. Kirby stood up with the rest of the students, but he moved off to the side to get out of the way. He watched but didn't participate. I moved over where he was standing and tried to connect. Withdrawn, he wouldn't even glance at me.

Class ended, and as the students lined up at the door to leave, I grabbed his classroom teacher. "Can we talk about Kirby?" I asked. "Don't worry about him," she said. "You can just put him off to the side if he's causing trouble." With that, she was gone.

I sat down at my desk and wrote Kirby's mom a note. I told her that Kirby didn't participate in class, and I wanted to know what I could do to encourage him. Over the course of the week, she wrote back and told me that she and Kirby would be talking about music class at home to prepare him. She thought it might help him get ready for the change in environment.

When Friday rolled around, I was giddy with anticipation of my second-grade double class. I had read up on students with Asperger's. From the information I had found on the Internet, it seemed that such students responded to physical touch and tangible tasks. My lesson used group movement with partner motions. I was hoping that Kirby would like interacting with his peers. Unfortunately, when it came time to find a partner, Kirby was left standing alone, looking more sullen than ever. I rushed over to him and became his partner. His motor skills were rough, and he seemed frustrated not to be able to meet my motions as the song required. A few of the other students saw that Kirby couldn't do the simple movements and they started to make fun of him. I flashed them my best teacher look and the comments stopped as fast as they had started. I couldn't tell if Kirby had noticed the comments, though, or if they had hurt his feelings.

Continuing for the first quarter of the school year, I tried out various lessons and techniques to get Kirby involved in music class. We'd been learning about rhythm and using our bodies to clap and tap simple rhythm patterns I had notated on the board. It was time to apply our new knowledge to playing instruments. I had been building up this special activity for a few weeks, and the students were excited. All the instruments were lined up at the front of the room. In groups of four, students came up to the instruments, grabbed their mallets, and played the rhythm pattern on the board. It was harder than they thought it would be. It was a humbling experience for even the smartest kids in the class.

Kirby sat patiently waiting his turn. He was in the last group to play. The rest of the kids in class held their breath, waiting for Kirby to mess up or act out. But instead, the most amazing thing happened: Kirby played the rhythm perfectly! Claire, a little girl sitting close to Kirby, was the first student in the class to notice how well he played.

"Mrs. Hare! Watch Kirby, he's so good!"

I had noticed and was just as excited as Claire. I wrote a new rhythm on the board, and Kirby played it perfectly again. The class applauded. With only five minutes remaining in class, I continued to write rhythms on the board so Kirby could play them. The class was encouraging him and I was proud of both Kirby and the class's positive affirmation. But best of all, Kirby smiled. It was the first time I had seen him show any emotion. His body was almost bouncing with excitement. He looked around at his peers with a huge grin on his face. They approved of something he had done, and you could tell it made him feel special and accepted.

When it was time to line up for dismissal back to his home room, Kirby hugged me.

I sat down at my desk to write his mother a note about how gifted Kirby had been at playing rhythms in class that day. In return, I got a note that I still have and treasure almost 10 years later. In it, she thanked me for taking the time to find a way to reach Kirby. More importantly, she was touched that I had called Kirby "gifted." It was a label she thought might never be associated with her son. Among the usual notes sent home to her about things Kirby couldn't do, this one positive affirmation meant a great deal to her.

I had the pleasure of teaching Kirby until the fifth grade. And while he had a different classroom teacher every year and faced challenges to keep up academically, my music class served as a safe haven for him. The hug he gave me that day was just the first of many.

Ryan's Fragility

Jan Hasler

L IFE TAKES STRANGE twists and turns, most certainly in the field of education. In my quest to be a lifelong learner, understanding the syndrome called "fragile X" presented a real challenge. The word *fragile* intrigues me, as signifying something delicate and precious. Ryan was all that and more.

I had been teaching for many years in what we referred to as "normal" or "regular" classes. No one said it was easy. In fact, it's still the norm to have more than a handful of reading and comprehension levels in one classroom. Likewise, the time frame for a particular child's learning is anything but regular and consistent with the rest of the class. Unfortunately, many children fall through the cracks and proceed through life without ever reaching their learning potential. This particular year Ryan was on the edge of falling.

I had just transferred to a new building and was filled with excitement for this school year. My boards were decorated, but I hadn't received my roster of students. When I saw the principal saunter in with a look of doom, I didn't know what to expect. He proceeded to explain that a teacher in the special education department had had to resign, suddenly. Would I consider incorporating her students into my classroom? I would have an assistant who had experience dealing with special-needs students. I would have fewer students than the "regular" classes. To top it off, these 11-to-13-year-olds would switch classrooms for elective classes and would be served weekly by occupational and physical therapists. Could I refuse such a deal? Besides, I would make some points with a new principal.

Surely I had to seek some advice before accepting this tempting offer. It came quickly, without my asking, delivered by our school district's special education supervisor. I became the student and she the teacher. She presented me with numerous reading materials that pertained to each child's diagnosis. The umbrella impairment was autism, which can exhibit a wide range of characteristics from minor to severe. I eventually studied each child's IEP (individual education plan) with separate parent and child meetings. The emotional connection, or twist in the road, had been made. There was no chance for turning back now.

So it began, and the excitement certainly started. As his mother and younger sisters proceeded down the hallway that first day, Ryan lagged far behind. We weren't sure he'd ever be coaxed into the classroom. If he saw us looking his way, he'd turn and do an unbalanced shimmy in the opposite direction. This became his little game. He sure was cute with his flapping hands, large ears, and clomping feet, which are common characteristics for the gene mutation called fragile X. But dealing with his screaming hysterics wasn't cute. Our salvation that first day was some colored blocks and a secluded desk that shielded Ryan from the rest of the class. We had to maneuver without a lot of touching, due to Ryan's negative responses.

The diverse makeup of this class actually helped to expand the overall sensitivity for others that would have been hard to teach any other way. Some students understood the necessity to be patient with one another. Others were terribly distracted by a student that they thought was allowed to do whatever he wanted in a separate corner of the room. How do you justify asking all the rest to behave, while one doesn't have to? Two mentally impaired girls took comfort in sitting close and working together. They cried if you asked them to work independently. Another thought everything was funny and proceeded to laugh out loud for most of the day. Did I feel stressed? Without a doubt, I did. My teaching assistant lent some relief when I needed a break, until the day came when I had to say to her, "No way, stop!"

After a few days, Ryan became accustomed to the routine of coming into the classroom and immediately going to his station with the colored blocks. I had managed to work one-on-one with him to incorporate simple counting and matching activities, using these blocks. Ryan's demeanor with me became less antagonistic than it was with my assistant. Her patience was beginning to wane where Ryan was concerned. She repeatedly told me that she had experience with "these types." I questioned whether you could put children like Ryan, or any child, into a classified type.

As my assistant pushed Ryan to adhere to her expectations, he backed off more. At times he would throw a tantrum, kicking and throwing things as he screamed. Of course we had to separate him from the rest of the class and give him reasonable, disciplinary consequences for his actions. Although he demonstrated the cognitive tendencies of a five-year-old, he had the strength and size of his chronological age, 11 years. My approach was to let him rage when he needed to vent but to prevent him from hurting himself or others. On the day when my assistant felt it best to attempt to hold him down while he kicked and screamed, I stepped in and said, "No way, stop!"

Ryan and my assistant were startled but calmed down quickly. I can't say everything went smoothly after that, but at least the ground rules were set for who was boss in this classroom. I began to ask my assistant to teach certain areas of the curriculum to the rest of the class while I spent the time working with Ryan. His delayed speech and language development slowly began to improve. He also learned to trust me, and he smiled as he mastered a new concept. To improve his attention span, I ultimately used his blocks as a reward system when he stayed on task for longer periods of time.

The big day came when we ventured out into the halls of our school. The social and emotional impact was powerful. Ryan didn't like the confusion of changing classes with all the other students in the hallways. They would often look at our students and whisper what would appear to be unkind remarks. Our "happy girl" would continue to laugh. The "regular students" weren't quite prepared for this response. We'd all end up laughing, which was good for our souls. At times Ryan took comfort in strutting down the hallways, locking his arm in mine. This connection progressed into his wanting me to stay with him at special classes, like music and PE. It took some time for him to accept that I would leave when I felt he was safe and would return to pick him up later.

This slow, progressive approach didn't always sit well with some of the teachers who taught Ryan's extra classes. They thought he would understand their direct manner of authority and orders. Often Ryan would run off from their classes, calling for me to return. Several times he escaped into the school halls, and I would be called to look for him. In the long run, they couldn't handle the stress any better than I.

Needless to say, everyone was pleased to see the final results of Ryan's turnaround. Toward the end of the second quarter, Ryan began reading sight words and short sentences, along with performing simple math. He began to participate in small group instruction for short periods of time. His favorite activities involved singing the repetitive songs that we used for educational purposes. As long as a consistent routine was followed, Ryan could be counted on to stay calm and pacified. Then the day came when I threw off Ryan's routine and caused some havoc.

My back gave out, and it required major surgery. I would be out of school for approximately six weeks. Who was going to handle Ryan? Who would even want to? My assistant was happy with her routine, teaching small groups within the classroom. We needed a substitute teacher, quick! Fortunately, a retired businessman who had been on the substitute list kindly volunteered to step in. All the children knew him from his past assignments in our department. Ryan was told ahead of time that I would be leaving. A strange and wonderful thing happened right around this time.

Ryan began to get cold in class and often asked to wear my sweater. I would give it to him for short periods of time but made him give it back before changing classes. Once he proudly paraded down the hallway with it on. The onlookers thought this was quite amusing. When I told his mom about this occurrence, she quickly sent in extra clothes for Ryan.

Finally the day came when I had to leave for surgery. Of course I worried about my students and called often to check on them. I wasn't surprised to hear that Ryan was asking to wear my sweater more and more. He was content most of the time, as long as his routine was not interrupted. At other times he would want to lie down on the floor and cuddle up to this sweater. I too took comfort in knowing that a part of me was still there watching over Ryan.

When I returned to school, a new sweater was waiting for me, purchased by Ryan's mom and dad. I knew I couldn't ask for mine back and really didn't want it anyway. Ryan continued to progress, and ended the year reading on a second-grade level and doing first-grade math problems. Everyone, including the principal and doubting staff, was amazed at Ryan's accomplishments. Another school in our district was designated the following year for special needs students, so Ryan was transferred. We said our goodbyes with some hugs interspersed. I was proud to see him walk off and not look back. Actually, I didn't think I could hold my tears if he turned around.

Two years later I received an unexpected, unforgettable surprise. On my school desk was a package, wrapped in brightly colored paper with a big bow and a smiley-face card. I opened the package to find my worn sweater and a message that read, "Mrs. H, thanks for the use of your sweater. I went to my first homecoming dance with a date. I don't need the sweater anymore. You see, I'm not FRAGILE any longer. Ryan"

It's for these moments that we teach. All our students are fragile in one way or another. May you have many Ryans in your teaching career. Keep watch for those twists and turns that come your way. You may just find that they're blessings in disguise.

THE SQUARE DUDE

Sam Janeway

ALTHOUGH I'D HAD eight years of experience working with deeply disturbed students in residential
and day treatment settings, I was about to begin my first
teaching assignment in the public schools. My previous
schools taught only special education students. All of
those students had "blown out of" (been expelled from)
their public school (or schools), so they were segregated
and had no interaction with regular education students.
I was a little nervous because although the students I
would be teaching had to be able to function at a high
enough level to stay on a public school campus, there was
the added pressure that the administration, the teachers,
the regular education students (and their parents) were

always watching and expecting the worst. I like to call it the "fishbowl effect."

I was taking over a "special day class for emotionally disturbed students," which is the most difficult class to teach because the students' behaviors are often highly disruptive and can be unsafe if the class is not managed well. The teacher who had preceded me had quickly gained a reputation for not being in control of her class. As a result the school was not pleased with her, the class, or the students. When teachers found out which class I was teaching, they either made snide comments ("Good luck!") or cut the conversation short. I understood their frustration, and I also understood that it would weigh heavily on the students I would be teaching if I did not turn that perception around quickly. I had read the files on each of the returning students as well as the new incoming ones. In our district, special day classes for emotionally disturbed students had a class size of 10 students, as opposed to 35 to 40 in a general education class, because the emotionally disturbed students usually had severe emotional, home, and learning issues, and many of these students were "in the system" and lived in foster care or group homes. I knew going into my first day that I would be tested by at least one of my new students. Most teens will test a new adult to see how he will respond (a phenomenon called "substitute syndrome"). But students who are emotionally disturbed often do so as a survival mechanism because of past separations or traumas in their lives. The average student does it to gain a little attention or notoriety, while emotionally disturbed students usually test teachers to determine if they are safe. I kept that in mind as I waited anxiously for my students to arrive.

The first period that I taught was math, and as an icebreaker I asked students to say their name and something fun they did over the summer. Four students answered fairly appropriately, but when I got to the fifth (I'll call him Phil), he said, "I don't have to tell you shit, you square-ass bitch," and left the class. I heard some laughs and felt the eyes of the nine remaining students on me, as they waited to see how I would react. In my past schools this is where the whole class would erupt and you would spend the rest of the day reeling them back in. But I guessed public school was different, because after Phil's exit you could have heard a pin drop. I had been cussed at before, so I knew better than to show that I was upset, but the main problem was that I did not know the school's official procedure for such situations.

I skipped the rest of the introduction, pulled out the math textbook, and told the class to open up to the first lesson. A female student (Sarah) said insistently, "Aren't you going to write a referral?" I sensed by her tone that she was in earnest and not teasing, so I let her know that I intended to do so after class. That was an acceptable answer to the class and so we got to work. At the end of the period another student came up to me (Harold) and said, "You shouldn't let him talk to you that way." I asked him what he meant, and he said, "Everyone's watching, you know what I'm saying?" I did know what he was saying, and I appreciated that he was trying to help me, but there was nothing I could do because Phil was gone. I was familiar with the code of the street (don't let anyone disrespect you), but in my previous schools there had been less structure in handling discipline. There was no dean, no set procedure for addressing misbehavior, and teachers generally preferred to intimidate students rather than write a referral that probably wouldn't be followed up. But the reality was that Phil had acted so decisively and so quickly that I hadn't been able to respond in time. Although I taught for the rest of the day, my mind was preoccupied with ways that I could nullify Phil's brilliant preemptive strike. I knew that even though the nine students who were present were starting to accept me, it meant nothing if I didn't pull Phil back into the group.

Special day classes for emotionally disturbed students are self-contained classrooms, which means that the teacher has the same students for all four of their core classes (English, math, science, and history). Phil did not attend any of the other three classes he had with me. At lunch I looked up his address, and as soon as the final bell rang, I took the bus to his house. I knocked on the door, and his grandmother (his guardian) answered. I explained who I was and she invited me into the house. While we sat and talked, Phil's great-grandmother joined the conversation. After we had been sitting for about half an hour, Phil arrived. He froze in the doorway and looked first at his grandmother, then his great-grand-mother, then at me, and his jaw dropped.

"Mr. Janeway was just telling us how he likes to visit the homes of all his new students."

Phil nodded slowly.

"What's wrong, Phil? He just wanted to go over your first day."

"Go ahead, Phil," I said. "Tell them what happened. Or if you like, I can tell them."

Caught in a double bind, Phil blurted out what had happened. His grandmother made him apologize. Then she turned to me and said, "Feel free to come by any-time, Mr. Janeway."

The next day Phil was on time to class and almost perfectly behaved. From that point on he was a model student, and to my delight the rest of the class followed suit. When they saw that my class was under control, other teachers actually began talking to me. My first year teaching Phil was his junior year. He was very bright but had earned only a 0.83 GPA the previous year. I thought he could do much better. At the start of the semester I gave all my students a general assessment to gauge their levels in math and language arts. Phil was exceptional in math, so I focused on building his self-esteem through his strongest academic area. I gave him more advanced work than his peers, and I also had him tutor the ones who struggled with math. He even started to make an effort on his writing assignments. Phil's GPA began to improve, so that after the first grading period he had earned a 2.00 (C average). He was beginning to take his schoolwork more seriously, and he stopped playing around in the halls between classes. In the beginning I had to go to the stairwell where he hung out every day between classes and walk him to class. He pretended to be irritated because his friends were watching, but I knew he appreciated it.

Phil came to me after the first marking period grades came out with a troubled look on his face. He told me that he had always wanted to play football but had never had the grades. Now that he had earned the required 2.00 GPA, he wanted to know if I thought he should try out even though the season had already started. Our relationship had grown to the point where I could tease him a little.

"You're asking a 'square-ass bitch' if you should play football?"

"Come on, man, you know what I'm saying."

"OK, OK. Are you any good?"

"Yeah, I was an all-star in Pop Warner. I've got good hands."

"What position do you play?"

"Tight end, outside linebacker."

"Go talk to the coach."

"I already did. They need a tight end."

"Then do it."

"All right, man, thanks."

I didn't let him see it in my face, because I didn't want to embarrass him, but that was the first time he had said thank you without my having to prompt him. When I'd first met him, he was a scared, angry, rude boy, but now he was starting to treat others with respect, and I knew that that was impossible to do without his first beginning to respect himself. In half a season Phil went on to make All City, and by the end of the year his GPA was a 3.50. I attended every home game.

At the end of the year, he asked me if he could take a regular class for his senior year. I told him he was going to have to work hard, and I put him in a regular-track math class. He would bring his homework to me, but besides that he did fine and earned a B+. There were some bumps at first, because he had to test his new (male) teacher. But I immediately called a conference with Phil, the new math teacher, and Phil's grandmother so that Phil would see that everyone was on the same page and that the new math teacher deserved the same respect as his grandmother or me. I reminded him that he had asked for that particular class. After that he was a model student in math class. When I would look in on him, he didn't stand out like some of my other students did who took regular classes.

His senior year, Phil was very focused and began to talk to me about college. In the past he had said,

"College is for suckers," but now he was interested. His weakest area was writing. I told him that he needed to improve his ability to write essays, which he did. He made All City for the second year in a row in football and his GPA when he graduated was 3.85. He came up to me at the end of the year, at graduation, an event that he had not necessarily expected to attend when I met him.

"I never had a teacher come to my house. How did you know that was going to work?"

"I didn't."

"Then why did you do it?"

"I knew that was the only way you'd hear me."

"You're probably right."

"Phil, just because you're graduating doesn't mean you can't stay in touch. After all, I know where you live."

He smiled and gave me a hug. "You're all right for a square dude."

I'll never forget my interactions with Phil because the unstated factor was that he wanted a positive male figure in his life. I knew he couldn't come out and say that, so I had to intuit it. He had the skills to succeed; he just wanted some support. When he cussed me out, I could feel that he wanted me to chase him. I also knew that chasing him immediately would be ineffective, because he would have been calling the shots and would not have heard my words. Showing up at his house unannounced, in the company of his primary caregiver, got his attention. Focusing on his strengths in order to help him build his self-esteem kept it. He played linebacker in college and graduated. Phil, now 25, works for the Sheriff's Department and still calls me to check in. There were other students whom I reached in my first public school class over the course of the year. But I knew that there was a very small window of time in which to reach Phil. I knew intuitively that in his particular case, I had to gain his respect before I could begin to help him with his academics. Looking back on it, I think we are both lucky we ran into each other when we did.

FROM STATION TIME TO MOTHER'S DAY:

TALES OF TEACHING FIRST WORDS

Amber Mackenzie Taylor

I AM ENTERING MY third year of teaching prekinder-garten and kindergarten for children with autism, my fifth year of working with students with special needs. Each time I start to feel hopeless I get a little gift, a greeting from a nonverbal student or a smile from an unfriendly colleague. These gifts most often come from our students and almost always come when we are least expecting them: a nonverbal child uses a new phrase or reaches out for help or makes his first joke. I've started a mental list of those moments to hold me together on the extra-long days when I end up wearing Cheerios in my hair to the assembly or realize after returning from the fire drill that I still have finger paint on my face. I collect those gifts and savor them. Today I want to share four of those moments, memories of children who have taught me to always expect the impossible.

My first year teaching children with autism, I began with just a few students, no classroom supplies, and a lot of books on instructional strategies, diagnosis categories, and writing individual education plans. My first student was Janelle, a five-year-old girl who loved Daisy Duck. Janelle could not yet write her name but she could draw picture-perfect scenes from the cartoon, complete with "© Disney," including the swirly *D*. Each time we attempted an instructional activity, she would fling the supplies across the room. If the carpet was off-center in our play corner, she would stand screaming, staring at the offending corner. We continued to practice language drills, attempt handwriting, and focus on language request strategies. More and more she began to attempt simple sentences and yet could never quite muster language in a time of crisis—until one day when she was in the middle of a tantrum. I sat down next to her on the floor and, more out of frustration than an attempt to communicate, said, "What do you want?" She sat up and shouted between sobs, "I . . . want . . . pick a station." I have never offered a child so many choices in my life. When I saw her an entire year after she had left my room, she approached, looked at me, and said, "Hi, teacher," clapping her hands as she spoke.

After I'd been teaching for a few months, Isaac started in my classroom, holding a matching block in each hand and screaming for hours at a time. He screamed anytime we changed activities, anytime we asked him to participate, and especially anytime we asked him to set down one of his matching blocks. When we sat at the art table coloring or painting, he would bend over under the table and rhythmically tap the table legs. We continued to present each activity, reviewing strategies for transitions, walking him over to his picture schedule, and talking with him about the activity we had finished and what was coming next. We modeled how to engage in each activity, making countless paintings to show him how to paint and placing the paintbrush in his hand between screams. After almost six months in my class, he was hospitalized to address some ongoing medical needs, and as he recovered from treatment, he began using phrases to ask about school. Looking up from his hospital bed, he would say, "I'm at school," the way we do each morning during attendance, and he would repeat, "Check schedule," as we do each time we start something new. When I called that week to see how he was doing, his mother's voice cracked as she told me that he missed us. When he left the classroom two years later, he had long forgotten his matching blocks and had begun writing his name, painting, and using language like "Come get me" to ask us to chase him on the playground.

Nearly a year later, Alana came to school for her first day with her hands full, literally. Everywhere she went, she carried a blanket, a toy car, and a pacifier. As she walked around the classroom and the playground, her blanket trailed behind; and she kept both eyes glued to her blanket everywhere she went. Over the course of several months we slowly earned her trust, asking her to place the objects on her lap, then on the table, then on the far side of the table, then on a separate table, and so on, until finally she was able to leave them in her cubby. Relieved that the months of screaming for these comfort objects had finally come to an end, we were satisfied to watch as Alana settled into a routine of placing all three objects in her cubby each morning. Then one day, completely on her own, she turned to her father during drop-off and said, "Here you go," handing over all her coveted objects as she ran onto the playground. After separating from her blanket, her car, and her pacifier, she began to explore the classroom, climb the play structure, and watch her peers. We saw for the first time that she has two beautiful bright brown eyes.

That spring Julian began in our classroom just days after his third birthday. He was stereotypically autistic in several ways, lining up his blocks, spinning the wheels of our toy cars, and screaming anytime we transitioned to a new activity. But first and foremost he could not tolerate anything messy, sticky, or dirty. He hated Play-Doh, avoided paint, and only ate pureed food heated to 72 degrees. Each day we presented an art project encouraging him to color, paint, cook, and get messy. Each day he would touch the objectionable substance as we insisted that he did and then promptly wipe his hands on whatever was most readily available: the table, the wall, his hair, me, whatever it took to get the mess off his hands. Julian would then politely but urgently insist, "Wash hands, wash hands, wash hands." Gradually, over time, he was able to wait a few minutes before washing his hands, and yet he remained suspicious of anything potentially messy. Then Mother's Day rolled around and we set out to make handprints. Julian watched guardedly as we painted each of his classmates' hands. When everyone else had finished, I sat down with Julian, telling him quietly that first it was "teacher's turn" and then it was his turn. I slowly painted each of my hands and made my handprints, explaining to him that we were putting paint on our hands to make a picture for Mommy and then we would wash them. When I had finished, I turned to him saying, "Julian's turn." He did not scream or fuss but instead locked eyes with me and said, "Then wash hands." He sat calmly, never taking his eyes off me, as I painted his hands one at a time. His mom called crying the following Monday, saying she had never seen his handprints before.

Next time you find yourself wearing art supplies as makeup or exhausted from an unsuccessful lesson, remember Janelle requesting station time, remember Isaac looking up from his hospital bed asking to check his schedule, remember Alana handing over her blanket, and remember Julian's first handprints, and remember to expect the impossible.

WHICH FRACTION DOES THE ALLIGATOR EAT?

Elisabeth Berkson

"SHUT UP, STUPID! Leave me alone! I hate you!" Sammy yells while he tears his paper in half, crumples it up, and throws it to the ground, along with his pencil and eraser. "Let's work on this one together," I had said just before he exploded, trying to help him correct a math problem. In his mind, he had failed. He could not deal calmly with the frustration he felt. He was angry at me and himself. His aggravation had boiled to the surface and erupted once again. Unfortunately, this is a typical day in math class for Sammy.

I teach special education. Most of the students in my class (ages six to nine, grades one to four) attend the school where I teach because their primary disability is emotional disturbance. Some students have other disabilities, including speech and language disorders, learning disabilities, and autism spectrum disorders. There are several teaching strategies I use to reach all the children, in addition to the ones that are specific to each learning difference.

Sammy has been in my class for a while—almost a year. He is a sweet, engaging student who likes positive adult attention. He is very athletic and enjoys playing outside. Academically, he has shown some improvement since joining the class; however, he has such low self-esteem in the classroom that he often gives up when the work seems too difficult or lengthy. As soon as he does a problem incorrectly or becomes distracted, he starts speaking in a baby voice and attempts to get his peers' attention in silly, inappropriate ways, such as whispering, making faces, or telling jokes to avoid continuing the work. This behavior becomes disruptive to the other students. He can't talk about difficult situations, his feelings, or his thoughts without using baby talk and attempting to avoid the conversation or changing the subject first. He starts to scan the classroom for an exit when he is feeling anxious, and he jumps at sudden noises made by his peers. Typically he becomes angry when asked to redo work. He crumples or rips his paper, calls others names, and throws things. These behaviors are not surprising, since Sammy lived in a physically abusive environment before his current placement. He also experienced neglect by his caregiver when he was younger.

To address these behaviors during math time, I often start the lesson with problems the students can do easily. After that, I teach the class a new concept, and while the other students are practicing either individually or in pairs, I sit with Sammy and reteach the lesson a few different ways. I do multiple problems with him to make sure that he understands. I praise every small accomplishment or attempt, to help bolster his self-esteem. I also present the problems one at a time so that he doesn't feel overwhelmed. We have worked together in this way since he joined my math group, working on mostly second- and third-grade skills although he is in fourth grade.

When preparing to teach my students, I choose the skills that I feel they will be able to learn and plan to teach them in a logical order. I research different strategies that could work for their learning abilities. One important skill is fractions. My fractions unit starts with studying symmetry (I love teaching symmetry because art can be incorporated in the lessons, including drawing and making collages). Next we look at identifying parts of the whole (this is one-eighth of a pizza, this is one-quarter of an orange, etc.), and then we learn to compare fractions. We had played several fractions games over the past few weeks and I felt confident that the students had the background skills needed for the next step and were ready to try something more difficult.

Today math begins like any other day. The students settle into their desks and I start teaching the new concept with something they all know—reviewing that the alligator mouth is hungry and it wants to eat the bigger number. The students remember this easily because they love to draw teeth in the alligator's mouth. Then I move into explaining the lesson on the board about eating the bigger fraction and we practice as a class. I do several examples, then call on each student except Sammy to answer a problem. I do not call on Sammy because he looks unsure, and once discouraged he usually stops paying attention and starts being disruptive. The other students begin to work on their own, and I sit next to Sammy. "OK! Let's do this!" I say. He looks at me, still confused, and picks up his pencil.

I explain again the ways you can figure out which fraction is bigger (I teach the students to cross-multiply the numerators and denominators and compare the answers or draw a picture to visually identify which is bigger) to find the answer. We start working together and do a few problems where I am guiding him to the correct answer. When I feel that he has more of a grasp on the concept, I give him a problem to do on his own. I write 1/2 and 3/4 on the page with a circle in the middle. He looks at it and I prompt him to draw a picture and try this one on his own. His circles are uneven, but the drawings are a clear representation of the difference. He draws the alligator mouth gobbling up the 3/4.

I feel excited that he seems to understand. "Way to go, Sammy! You did it! Are you ready to try another one?" I ask. He nods. I write 1/3 and 1/6 with a circle in the middle. He smiles and quickly draws the alligator mouth gobbling up the 1/6. "That's too easy," he says.

This is a moment when I have to carefully consider how I will respond. I do not want him to give up, but the answer is wrong so I have to correct him. What I say or do next could decide whether he continues with the problem or becomes angry and is finished with math for the day. I know that hearing he got the answer wrong can be frustrating for him, so I start to reach for his pencil to help him correct the problem. He looks at my face, reads that he has gotten it wrong, and then he snatches the paper away from me.

"I can do it," he says without looking at me. He knows he only has two other choices for the answer—the equals sign or the alligator mouth going the other way—but he also knows that I want to see his work. I take a deep breath and pull back my hand, unsure of what that voice tone means but encouraged by the words anyway. Inside my head, I am cheering. He wants to try again! He isn't giving up: today is already a success, even if the answer is wrong! He has never spoken that way after missing a problem. Typically, he gets angry, gives up, crumples the paper, gets distracted, and math is over for that day. I only have a short window of time to work one-on-one with him before the other students get distracted from their work, so I am hoping we've worked on enough problems together for him to understand.

"Great! Show me how," I reply, still not quite knowing what will happen next. I wonder what he is thinking. He sits for a few minutes that seem longer, staring at the problem. Then he draws the picture of the two fractions. The pencil is heavier on the page now, making thick indentations in the paper and threatening to break the lead. He is showing me that he is frustrated. He roughly colors in the pieces of the circle. I hold my breath, speculating on where this situation is going and hoping he gets the correct answer. The drawing is accurate, although messy and clearly the work of an agitated student.

He redraws the alligator mouth gobbling up the 1/3 and then looks carefully at my face to see how I respond to his answer. I am still holding my breath. "Is that right?" he asks me quietly.

I wait just one second and then grin. "Great job, Sammy!" I say. "You figured it out on your own and showed your work! I am so proud of you! Can I have a high five?" He draws his hand all the way back and slaps my hand hard. With my fingers still tingling, I give him a hug.

Sammy smiles. I write another problem for him and he starts to work right away.

■

SECTION FOUR

THE TEACHER BECOMES
THE STUDENT

IT'S WHAT YOU ANSWER TO

Susan DeMersseman, PhD

CHERI WAS ONE of the frequent fliers to my office.
As the school psychologist, my job was to deal with
all kinds of "problem kids." Cheri was one of my favorites. She was a sixth grader with more than one suspension in her short academic career. She was mouthy and
pugnacious, but also smart and honest. She usually got
in trouble for her retaliation to verbal taunts. She hated
to be teased, but she was not above bringing it on herself.

I believe that you shouldn't be working with children unless you're willing to learn from them. I think
there must have been a time when I thought I had all the
answers, but it didn't take long to learn that many of the

real answers were in the children. Cheri was one of my best teachers. She taught me two valuable lessons. The first was how important it is to cry with children when someone they care about is killed.

The community where I worked at the time was one in which most of the children knew someone who had died in a violent manner. The school was a fairly peaceful place, but the neighborhood was not. One weekend a 16-year-old boy who lived in Cheri's apartment building was shot and killed. He was one of the "good" kids and had always been nice to Cheri.

That Monday I got a call on the intercom from Cheri's teacher. She had become exasperated with Cheri and was sending the girl to my office. Cheri had been crying most of the morning and was unable to do any work. I was supposed to patch her up and get her back to class. For a minute I thought I should do that. I wanted to help out the teacher and get the child back into her studies. But then, thankfully, when I saw the girl, I was struck by good sense. Instead of trying to apply a quick bit of comfort and get her back to class, I sat and listened to her sadness and I cried with her. She stayed with me all morning. I did paperwork and stopped when she looked up from her book and wanted to talk.

How can a person not be moved by such an outrageous loss? I am certain that some of the rage we see in youngsters is a reaction to unresolved grief, to sadness to which no one has responded. Over the years of working with kids, it has become clear to me that many young-sters, particularly boys, transform sadness into anger and violence. Perhaps that response feels less weak and powerless than the sadness does.

Looking back, I am grateful that I had the common sense to respond to Cheri's sadness in a natural way. I hoped that being comforted and having her sadness understood would make her a more gentle person. I hoped that someday she might show similar compassion to someone else.

The risk, which I understand even better now, is that to minimize the sadness or the distress over such an event only conveys to a youngster that this event is somehow acceptable or OK. That human life is expendable. Instead we need, with every opportunity we have, to convey the preciousness of every life—the lives of people our students care about and the lives of people with whom they might be in conflict. Cheri taught me that just because some-thing is common, we cannot let it become acceptable.

In my year of working with Cheri, I learned another valuable lesson from her: a new way to deal with teas-ing. Each week she and I worked on some new coping strategy to keep her from overreacting and getting sus-pended again. For such an ornery kid, she was very thin-skinned. One week I shared something I had heard many times. "It's not what they call me. It's what I answer to." It sounded so lofty and poetic, I thought it might have some impact on the girl. She clearly understood the point of my phrase, but she was a step ahead of me. "Yeah," she responded, "that's like what my mom says, 'If they called you a truck, you wouldn't grow wheels.'" It hit the mark perfectly, and it was much better than what I had told her. It made me laugh and made Cheri happy that I liked her idea. I knew Cheri's mom, and could imagine this gritty lady just throwing it out after some statement like "Shake it off!"

In that one little phrase was a truth that, if understood, could keep many kids out of pointless conflicts and violence. It never feels good to be called names, but the words of others have *no* power to make us into what we are not.

The children I have worked with who are most vulnerable lack that understanding and, to make things worse, often lack a sense of self-worth. But even with those two qualities, young people are much more resilient and less likely to get into conflicts to prove their worth—often with people who couldn't see their worth anyway. (And both of those qualities are ones that we in schools can affect.) If youngsters know and believe that they are of value, then being called a truck or anything else will not have the same impact.

I have shared the words of this wise young girl many times. Her story led me to create a classroom activity on teasing, in which kids make up their own versions of Cheri's insightful statement. The students have created some sensible and some silly parallels:

"If they called you a tree, you wouldn't grow leaves."
"If they called you a bird, you wouldn't be able to fly."
"If they called you a Popsicle, you wouldn't melt."

Regardless of how zany the items, the activity helped even young children neutralize some of the power that unkind words might have. My year working with Cheri opened my eyes to the lessons I could learn from children, and they were lessons I was then able to share with other children. Sometimes we adults are on the receiving end of teachable moments—if we're paying attention.

GETTING ANOTHER CHANCE

Katherine A. Briccetti, PhD

"LET GO OF me, you stupid white Chinese lady."

I've been called a honky and a white bitch by raging children, but never a stupid white Chinese lady. I want to smile despite the situation.

Rodney's wrists are so slender I can grip both in one hand. A minute ago, when I moved a chair he was about to topple, the first grader slugged me, his kiwi-sized fists pounding on my forearms in a frenzy.

I can soothe children with blood streaming from gashes in their chins, make parents comfortable enough to uncross their arms and tell me their stories, and ease the pain of children who are grieving more losses than I will ever know. Some days I feel like Super School Psychologist, but this is not one of them.

Rodney breaks free of my grasp and begins to pummel me again. He's not strong enough yet to hurt me, and the fervor of this little boy's anger doesn't even shock me anymore. He's not the first child to call me a ridiculous name, to take a swing at me, to rage as if he were fighting a war. I simply need to convince him to walk a hundred yards to the office with me, so he can calm down, so we can figure out what's wrong. He's still screaming, and despite the carpeted hallway, his shouts are bouncing off walls and reverberating through the building. Classroom doors are closing one by one. On the bulletin board next to him, children's artwork—paintings and bold crayon drawings—is on display, and I notice that a picture of children playing jump rope has been ripped in half.

"Leave me alone, you—you stupid, stupid idiot," he shouts.

"Rodney, you have a choice," I say. "You can walk with me to the office without hitting me, or I can hold you until you calm down."

"Shut up!" He lands another punch, this one on my hand. This one smarts.

There's an adult-sized chair in the hallway, a heavy, wooden remnant from earlier days, its seat cracked down the middle, and I lead him to it, praying the cleft won't pinch my rear end when I settle onto it. I pull him onto my lap, wrapping my arms around his trunk, pressing his crossed arms to his chest.

"I see how mad you are," I whisper between his shouts, my lips close to his ear. "And maybe you're sad or scared too. You can talk to me about it if you want to."

The last child who threw tantrums like this at school had witnessed his stepfather punching his mother after returning home from the bar. When I met that boy's mother on our treeless, asphalt-covered playground after school and offered her my card, she grabbed his hand and stalked off, hollering at me over her shoulder, "We don't need any of your damn help."

"You can come to the office and color a picture," I say now to Rodney, wondering what his life has been like so far. "Would that help make you feel better?"

"Let go of me, you ugly thing."

He screams as if I'm beating him, and I glance around, searching for backup, but the teachers are busy with their classes. It would be just my luck to have the district superintendent drop by for a visit right now. On second thought, it might be good for him to see what the school staff has to contend with. How difficult it has become to teach in urban schools, even in one like this— not in a ghetto but in a working-class neighborhood of Asians, blacks, Latinos, and whites.

I speak to Rodney in a measured tone, even though my pulse is thrashing in my ears. "When you're ready to walk to the office with me," I say, "we can get up."

He screams again, pulls his leg forward, and aims for my leg. I don't see it soon enough, and his sturdy little boot crashes into my shin.

I gasp and wrap my leg around both of his so he can't fire off another kick. We must look like a human pretzel entwined on this antique school chair, white and brown limbs entangled.

Years ago, when I worked with multi-handicapped children—kids with mental retardation, emotional problems, *and* behavior disorders—I was trained in safe restraint methods, in order to keep both child and adult from getting hurt. I've done this only a half-dozen times in my 20 years as a school psychologist, and I have always walked away with at least a bruise or two, sometimes scratches, and a couple of times, bite marks. But the child is unharmed.

Rodney is a runner—a child who takes off from class and roams the playground or, worse, heads off down the street. We are one block from a major thoroughfare, three from the freeway. We used to have a burly campus supervisor, a gentle man with an athlete's physique, who would pick up a child like Rodney and carry him under his arm like a football to the office. But we lost him in the last round of budget cuts, and it's up to me to get Rodney to a place where he'll be safe.

Rodney's teacher appears at her doorway. She's a young Chinese American who's taken extra classes to learn about challenging children. "I can get Mrs. Harris on the intercom," she says.

Principal Harris—an African American woman 10 years my senior—and I have guided many children to the office, dodging blows and verbal attacks. Each year we have seen more angry, frustrated children, and each year they are younger. We have witnessed kindergartners hurling chairs across the room, slugging other five-year-olds in the face.

I should be able to handle this little guy myself. I have a bunch of degrees and am no rookie. In most districts, school psychologists travel among several schools and provide only special-education testing, but this elementary school uses a portion of its budget for my counseling services one day a week. I want to earn my keep and don't want to let them down. Plus it's what I enjoy most about my job. Through the years I've calmed scores of explosive children—just by listening and trying to understand, empathizing, and problem-solving. Most kids secretly long to be contained, even physically like I'm doing with Rodney, because it's scary to feel so out of control. Often the children who start off the rockiest, like this boy, are the ones who end up bonding with me the strongest. But now I simply feel ineffective. This isn't working, and I'm not sure what else I can do.

"Yes, please," I say to Rodney's teacher. I feign calm while holding Rodney, still thrashing, on my lap. But she doesn't have to call the principal on the intercom.

Mrs. Harris is headed this way right now with her men-tee, a young teacher with aspirations of becoming an administrator. Why, I often wonder, would anyone *want* to be a principal? A principal's job is like an NBA ref-eree's during playoffs, taking heat from all sides.

Rodney wiggles in my lap, still fighting. "Stupid bitch," he screams.

"Rodney, sweetie," Mrs. Harris uses her sugar voice. Since Rodney enrolled at our school only a week ago, we don't know him well. With some kids she uses her principal voice: she shouts once to get their atten-tion, then demands they knock it off and get with the program. "Honey, come with me to the office so you can calm down."

I release my grip and he stands between us, muscles tensed. Fight or flight.

"Come on now, let's go."

Mrs. Harris grasps his wrist and he crumples to the floor. He will not budge. I hold his other wrist and take a step. He stands but braces his feet in front of him like a bull resisting the pen.

"Rodney, come with us," Mrs. Harris's principal voice seeps through. "I'm going to call your mother, and you can talk to her." This finally breaks his resolve, and tethered between us like laundry on a line, he begins to shamble toward the office, still hollering.

Halfway there he turns, gaping at me as if he has just realized, *You're still here?* His scrunched-up face is full of disdain, and before I know it's coming, a mouthful of spit the size of a garden slug is wobbling on my bare forearm.

I'm stunned. I have been spit at before, but never has it landed so perfectly on my bare skin. Without thinking—the urge to get it off me is so strong—I wipe Rodney's saliva on the back of his sweater. For the first time, I notice his new clothes are all a size too big, probably so he can wear them longer. The navy pants' cuffs drag on the floor and he's grabbing the waistband in back to hike the pants up. His bright white shirttails spill over his beltless middle, making him look all the smaller.

When he feels me wipe my arm onto the back of his sweater, he yells again, "Stupid white lady."

Mrs. Harris glares at him. "You shouldn't have spit on her."

When we arrive at her office, I peel off and let Mrs. Harris take him to call his mother. Later I hear that when he picked up something from her desk and she took it back from him, he kicked her on the shin.

A week before the winter school holiday, Rodney's mother, Ronette, calls me. Their apartment has been broken into and all their Christmas presents stolen. It's the third time in a year they have been burglarized. The time before Rodney's mother surprised the intruder and he assaulted her. Now Rodney can't sleep at night, and he's pounding holes in the walls. Ronette cries as she relates this, and I find myself fighting my own tears.

"I'm so sorry," I say, thinking of the presents for my own children under our tree, in our safe neighborhood.

Ronette has called one of the psychotherapists I recommended and will take Rodney for another session this week. But for now his outbursts in school continue. Some days she must come sit with him so he doesn't run off. When I visit his classroom and help his table with an art project, he refuses to look at me. When I say hello to him at lunch, he ignores me. While most kids love to come to my office to color pictures and talk, he still shuns my offers. He and I have not bonded, and this saddens me. I worry that I'm losing my touch.

I can't stop thinking about this family with no Christmas presents under their tree, so the day before school lets out for the winter break, I phone a local charity and share Rodney's family's story. The man in charge of the holiday toy giveaway invites me to come and pick out toys for Rodney and his four-year-old sister. It is storming when I make my trip downtown, and when I finish choosing toys, I scramble to my car carrying the gifts in plastic garbage bags while dodging giant puddles, but I am oddly happy. It finally feels like I am doing something to help.

"Thank you so much," Ronette says, tearful again, when I hand her the bag of gifts the next day. Her tiny, fenced-in yard is immaculate, and the windows—encased behind bars—glisten in the sunlight. "The kids will be so happy."

I enjoy her appreciation more than I should, maybe because it is so rare in this job. I didn't sign on to the job for back-patting and praise, though. I wanted to work at something that changed people's lives, give back something from my life of privilege. That, I believed, would be gratifying enough. But now there are times when a brief acknowledgment like this keeps me going.

In a reversal of roles, Rodney taught me something. I cannot heal every child. And since working with him, I've come to accept that if I can make a few children's lives in some way less burdened, a little less filled with grief and outrage, it will be enough. The kids have so many things working against them—a parent in jail or abusing drugs, cousins and siblings killed in drive-by shootings, poverty slowly suffocating their families. We see too much bottomless grief turning into eruptions of rage. How can children learn when they can't stop worrying about what might happen to their families, to them?

Still, I am optimistic about Rodney's future. I consider the system, which often fails kids, and then think of the people working within that system who have contributed something to Rodney and his family: a caring teacher, an accessible principal, a generous charity, and a battle-weary school psychologist. But I believe it is his mother who deserves most of the credit. Because of her, I believe Rodney has a chance. And I am grateful to her for showing me that I might have done enough.

I have only a minute to mull over my moment of clarity before someone knocks at my door. "Excuse me, Kathy," the principal says, poking her head in to my office. "Can you come with me?" I join her on a walk down the hall to a third-grade classroom. "There's a child in this class," she whispers as she opens the door, "who needs you."

THE FIELD TRIP

Rosemary Taylor

M Y YEARS IN Seattle preschools brought many adventures, but my favorite was the field trip to the waterfront with the four-year-olds.

Field trips are always a big deal, as there is so much to do before you can leave the building. First, the questions:

Does the place that you want to go allow your
   age group?

Do they have a tour?

Are there bathrooms?

Is there parking?

Is there a place for a large group to eat?

If it rains, is it covered?

Can we get parent drivers?

Are they properly insured?

Do we have permission slips and driver requests
   to send home?

So I called the fire station on the waterfront and they
told me that they had a tour of the boat, or we could
come see them test their hoses and that they would have
a hat for each child. I said I thought the hose testing
would be best and reserved the day.

Then I called the ferry building to see if we could
tour the ferry terminal and if there was a short ride we
could take. No short ride, but we could go aboard the
boat via the second-floor walk-on ramp while cars were
unloading. Great. I set the time and date and moved on
to a place to eat.

I called Ivar's, a great fish-and-chips restaurant right
next to the fireboats that has lots of hungry seagulls as
well as tables, covered and uncovered, outside. Ivar's
asked that we avoid the Friday lunch rush and thanked me
for calling ahead. The trip was set for the last Thursday
of the month. Wow, now to put this all down on paper
and get it sent out to parents for help and permission.

Monday morning we began the classroom curriculum about the waterfront and sea life. We learned about
the firefighters who worked on the fireboats, and we

made fire hats from paper plates to wear home that day. The children took home their red permission slips and red car-shaped driver requests and information about what we would be doing.

For the next three weeks, our classroom had fireboats in the water table and ferryboats made from shoe boxes loaded with cars in the block area. We read books and talked about sea birds, boats, docks, and barnacles.

We painted gray, white, and black seagulls and hung them high from the ceiling, with jellyfish—made from blown-up sandwich bags and strips of tissue paper, with a rubber band to keep the jellyfish nice and round— hanging below.

The permission slips returned and driver requests were filled as the excitement grew about our trip to the waterfront. We made car assignments and color-coded the name tags. Lunches would all go in a color-coded box in each car. I packed a first-aid kit and list of children for each driver, along with directions for parking and where to meet if separated.

Teachers, parents, and students were ready. Lunches in boxes, children in cars, and first-aid supplies and list and directions all handed out. We were ready.

The sky held the rain as our group crossed the street to see the fireboat test its hoses, and we walked safely on and off a ferry in our fire hats without having the ferry pull away with a child onboard. Seagulls were everywhere, and because of low tide we could even see barnacles on the pilings. I am not sure who had more fun, the adults or the children. After we ate our lunches at Ivar's and fed seagulls many pieces of bread, we prepared to return to school. A small hand tugged on my sleeve. I stooped down and said, "Yes, Jake."

"Miss Rosemary, I have a question: are seagulls and eagles made by the same company?"

To this day I am not sure what I answered, but I have never forgotten the question on that field trip. And I had thought I was so completely prepared . . .

The Good, the Bad, and the Crazy

Alistair Bomphray

I'VE GOT SOME crazy sophomores this year. The kids aren't disrespectful per se, they're just . . . young. And I actually kind of love them for it. Their transgressions have been more cute than they've been disheartening—with a couple of exceptions, of course.

Case in point: the time I found a dime bag of marijuana on the floor of my room. Even less cute was when Roberto tried to claim it after class. "What you gonna do with that?" he asked.

"I don't know," I replied, amazed that he was even *trying* this with me. His eyes darted back and forth between the little bag and the stunned expression that was surely writ across my face.

"Give it to me," he said, a Cheshire Cat grin taking away some (but not all) of the menace and strangeness from the request.

"Are you for real?" I asked. Dude was about one millitesticle (that's how male pattern boldness is measured, didn't you know?) away from reaching out and grabbing the bag from my hand, *and to hell with the consequences*. An awkward moment passed. Common sense won out at last and he booked it to lunch.

This is a kid who got into an altercation with a teacher last year while high on PCP. That's freakin' horse tranquilizer, if you didn't know. I wouldn't want to hang out on a beach in the Caribbean drinking margaritas while high on PCP, let alone sit through high-school math class. Roberto don't give a *damn*.

What I really mean to say is, yeah, my classes are a little crazy, but it's a lovable crazy, minus PCP-doing sociopaths. Even Roberto isn't a mean kid, just deeply misguided. Which I suppose would be an apt descriptor for a lot of my students. Or—even better—deeply *unguided*.

And I guess that's part of my job—to guide.

So it wasn't a surprise when my third-period sophomores crowded into my room last Friday and brought with them the unmistakable scent of good ol' California herb. Not as in somebody had sparked up a joint in there, but as in somebody had some fresh stinky stuff on his person. Which is to say, the smell wasn't going to go away. I knew it was bad when one of my seniors popped his head in the room and said, "Yo, what you *doooin'* in here, Mr. B?"

Getting high, I wanted to deadpan. *Whaddaya think?*

Instead I said, "Yeah, I know, it stinks," looking around the room meaningfully.

A teacher's daily life is made up of literally thousands of miniature forks in the road. And there's usually not time for extended deliberation. We must act quickly and decisively. Here I was at one of those forks: Do I make a big deal out of this? Or do I just move on?

Personally, I can't stomach the idea of calling security into my room to search backpacks. Nor do I want to accuse the wrong kid (which, by the way, happened to me once when I was in high school). So I acknowledged the smell (*If you thought we couldn't smell it, think again, dumb ass,* the implied message) and moved on.

This day was a little different, though. The assistant principal was scheduled to observe me, formally. The fact that my room smelled like a Method Man concert was mildly disconcerting, to be sure. But minus that annoying detail, I was ready for her: lesson plan printed out (check), materials all in order (check), student-centered activity ready to go (check), hair combed (well, that's not *that* important, is it?).

A few years ago I would've been freaking out. A freaked-out teacher is kind of like a really nervous car mechanic. You don't want that guy anywhere near your precious 1994 Corolla. And kids smell panic, you know they do. The quiet kids wrinkle their noses and think, *Oh, no,* while the Robertos either check out completely or circle in for the kill. This is why a teacher whose inner monologue reads something like *Oh damn oh damn oh damn* . . . ain't guiding *no one.*

Back when I started, it didn't even take a formal observation to freak me. The mere possibility of having an administrator walk into my room while things might look, in the language of the gods, "unsatisfactory" was enough to make me jumpy. Problem was, my conception of what my classroom *should* look like was completely made up of what I thought my administrators wanted to see—a lifeless, generic vision of the so-called model classroom that had very little to do with me as a teacher or a person.

One time when things got really bad (cue first-year teacher laugh track), I actually stood on my desk in a desperate attempt to take back my class. *Up here, please! Up here! I'm talking!* (C'mon, you know you've thought about it.) Ironically, an administrator did look into my room at that very moment, and for the rest of year I was known as that crazy new teacher who teaches standing on his desk. That's some kind of teachable moment, hey?

This neurotic impulse to snuff out anything perceivable as chaos in my classroom would stick with me into my fourth year. That was the year I was assigned the old auto shop space, i.e., a big high-ceilinged garage—complete with retro Valvoline sign on the wall and greasy engine parts spilling out of the closets—modified to look like a classroom, sort of. This was a space already given over to chaos: long, tentaclelike Shop Vac® hoses hung ominously from the ceiling; twin industrial-sized fans would sporadically turn on and drown out even my most inspired attempts to teach. In some essential way, I gave up on trying to make my class *look* perfect.

It helped that thanks to the out-of-the-way location of the garage—and perhaps to the fact that very few administrators even knew I was in there—my classroom became a kind of sanctuary, free from the prying eyes of clipboard-carrying principals. For the first time in my teaching career, I stopped worrying about how my class would look if someone official walked in the door. Relieved of this burden, I was finally able to relax into the kind of teacher I wanted—and therefore needed—to be.

Now in my sixth year, I'm a lot more confident in the face of evaluation. I don't feel the need to perform or to go out my way to please my evaluator. In other words, I'm not afraid of getting fired. I just want to be myself and not mess up in some major way—you know, like fart on a student or something.

In fact, I've grown kind of stubbornly opposed to changing my routine in any way for the benefit of administrators. I want them to see my class for what it is. *Yeah, it smells like weed in here. What can I say? These are my kids. Welcome.*

Adding a principal to the mix changes the kids' behavior too. Typically, this means for the better, and as a newer teacher I graciously benefited from this phenomenon. But I've gotten to the point in my career where I don't want to put on a show anymore, and I don't want my kids to either. I want it to be real.

I was not to be disappointed this time. My kids were absolutely, 100 percent themselves. They interrupted each other. They got distracted. They struggled to transition from one activity to the next. Two kids got in a yelling match. Another kid called his friend a *"pendejo."* They also participated. They said really smart things. They completed all the activities. They listened.

It was my most authentic evaluation ever. When the assistant principal left my room after 40 minutes of silently observing and typing on her laptop, I thought, *Well, she saw it all. The good, the bad, and the crazy.*

It strikes me now as I write this that perhaps one of the distinguishing characteristics of an experienced teacher (not that I'm anywhere near such hallowed ground yet) is simply being comfortable in one's own skin: as a disciplinarian, a teacher, an employee, and a human being. This doesn't mean not wanting or needing to become better, it just means being at peace with the way things are, even when things are kind of out of control. How much better prepared to gently guide

Roberto is the teacher whose real identity is not in conflict with his teacher identity?

When that yelling match broke out, the two-years-ago me would've thought, *You assholes! I'm being observed right now!* And then I would've frantically tried to break it up, a pitch of desperation in my voice. Perhaps I would've even tried to mediate the conflict, thinking that's what my principal wanted to see. This time I remained calm, cool even. "Anthony. Tricia," I said. "Can we move on?" And we did.

I haven't had my postobservation conference yet. I imagine it'll just be a formality: *Good job on this. Do better on that. Now sign on the dotted line.* Regardless, it seems a significant victory that I was able to be so *myself* up there, even when things didn't go exactly as I wanted. The important shift here, I think, is that my classroom is no longer a threatening place for me, crazy sophomores be damned. This is the opposite of saying that my classroom is my domain and that I'm the master of that domain or some such nonsense. It's saying that I've made a home of the chaos. And if I want to make a career out of this thing, I'd better learn to live in it.

TAMING THE WILD DINOSAUR

Rebecca Branstetter, PhD

M Y JOB IS to figure out how kids learn. As a school psychologist, I am often called to an array of different schools to test students, and I never know what I am going to encounter. Most of the time the kids are more than eager to bound off with a stranger to get out of class and get some one-on-one adult attention. They put forth their best effort and I happily test away, write up my results, and present to the teacher and parents how the student learns best and how to work with the student.

And then there was Max.

Max was a six-year-old boy who was in foster care,

and he was the teacher's nemesis. While she understood that his life was in turmoil, shifing from foster home to group home and back, he was not a student who could be easily contained. He was best described as a mini-tornado, whirling about the classroom, destroying all learning potential around him. The teacher, Ms. Jenkins, was an experienced woman who was doing everything in her power to contain him. She was at her wits' end. After doing a classroom observation, I couldn't blame Ms. Jenkins. Max was a force of nature.

I watched him during reading circle. While all the students sat on their spots on the rug, Max rolled around on his belly on the edge of the rug and sang to himself, "You should listen to the *teeeeacher,* the *teeeeeeacher.*" Ms. Jenkins tried peer pressure first: "I like the way Daniel is sitting crisscross-applesauce with his hands to himself." Twenty little ones took the hint and sat up even straighter with their little hands on their "crisscrossed-applesauced" legs, eager for praise. Max, however, got up and threw a pencil can across the room and looked at his teacher as if to say, *What are you going to do about that, lady?* Ms. Jenkins took a deep breath and said, "Max, please take a time out in the listening center for not being safe." Max looked right at her, pushed a rainbow of construction paper onto the floor, and screamed, "No!"

Ms. Jenkins got up from her lesson, put her hand gently on his shoulder, and said, "Why don't you go to your office and work there for a while." *Wait, this kid has an office? I don't even have an office at this school, being a nomad school psychologist and all.* But sure enough, there was a special little corner just for Max where he could work alone. He looked up at Ms. Jenkins, stuck out his tongue, and went to his "office," where he promptly crawled under the desk, curled into a ball, and began playing with a contraband dinosaur toy.

During all this, Ms. Jenkins had lost the attention of her first graders, who were now squirming, talking, and playing on the rug. Ms. Jenkins looked pleadingly at me, and I decided it was a fine time to take Max for testing.

I cautiously approached Max's office, crouched down, and asked him, "Do you want to go play some games with me?" Oh, how I love to trick the children into thinking cognitive assessments are "games"! Max, predictably, said, "No." I told him he had a choice: I could join him in his office or he could come with me to play games. Oh, how I love to trick the children into thinking they have a choice! This time, it worked. He agreed to go to the library for my "games." Unfortunately, as soon as he left the room, instead of going toward the library, he ran away from me in the opposite direction. I had a runner. Cursing myself for wearing heels that day, I took off after him with my three bags of testing materials. There should be some sort of School Psychologist Olympics for the sheer physical challenge of this job, never mind the mental challenge.

I caught up with Max at the basketball court out in the yard. As if this were always our intended destination, he said, "I'll go with you if you make this shot." This was another test. I had a decision to make. Did I bust out my teacher look and give a clear directive that it was not time for basketball but rather time for testing, or did I press my luck with my hideous basketball skills? I agreed to the physical challenge because I was afraid the little guy would take off again. I took the basketball and I thought of that old Easy Spirit commercial from the eighties where all those ladies play basketball in their pumps. It was my turn to play ball in heels. I took a deep breath, focused, and as if the testing gods had seen my ridiculously long caseload of students I had to get to today, I made a free-throw shot, for the first time in my life! I looked at Max expectantly and, I kid you not, he said, "You have to make two." I knew that the shot I had made was a total fluke, so I said in my most Pollyanna voice, "That one was worth two points. Here we go to the library!" Inside, I was growing frustrated. On the outside, I was trying desperately to be positive with Max.

Max didn't take the bait. He said, "No!" and ran back into the classroom before I could even protest. "Well, at least he didn't run away from school," the Pollyanna in me thought. I followed him back to a very confused but probably very validated Ms. Jenkins. If the school psychologist couldn't get Max to work, then who could? Max was back in his office, this time with his head on his table. I whispered, "Max. When you are ready to go to the library, I will be over there in the listening center." He growled, "No." I went to the listening center and waited. It wasn't long before Max joined me and together we tried again to make the long trek to the library. He liked being in charge. I couldn't blame Max, as so much of his life had been chosen for him. He had been given several different sets of foster parents and had little predictability over the most basic need of knowing who would be tucking him in each night and taking care of him the next day.

When we finally made it to the library, I immediately pulled out my most interesting "game," which was to make block designs. To add an element of "fun," the game was timed to see how quickly he could do it. It wasn't long before he was crawling on the table and the blocks were on the floor. I tried a drawing task. Max took the pencil, pointed at me, and said, "I have a pencil" in a threatening way. I knew Max was pulling for me to punish him. As a school psychologist, I know that many times foster kids who have been rejected in their lives or have experienced abandonment tend to try to "replay" a way to be rejected. Putting a pencil within inches of my eyeball would be one way to do that. I simply noted, "I wonder if you can use that pencil to draw a circle?" And he did. My eyeballs were safe. I thought I'd finally broken through with Max.

I tried to capitalize on his interest in drawing by

doing another drawing task with him. Kids love drawing, right? Max drew a picture of a big fat person with snot coming out of the nose and said, "Once upon a time, there was an old, old lady whose name was Dr. Branstetter, I mean, Dr. Fat. She got eaten by a monster, and so did her pen and timer." Well then. I wanted to defend my 30-year old, adequately body-mass-indexed self. Instead, I tried to engage him by stating, "I wonder what made the monster mad at Dr. Fat."

It was then that he jumped out of his seat and began crawling on the floor, snarling and snapping his jaws. Before I knew what was happening, he screamed, "I'm a dangerous, mean dinosaur!" and he *bit my ankle*. Well, I did not see *that* coming.

How far was my patience and unconditional positive regard going to have to go to work with Max? If I were a teacher, this guy would have been in the office in 2.2 seconds. Sadly, there just isn't time in a classroom of 20 to 30 kids to work with kids like Max in such a nondirective, therapeutic way. I had to shift my expectations as well. Even with the most cooperative student, my testing takes several hours. Since I was getting nothing out of Max just yet, I resigned myself to the fact that I was going to be here awhile. We had a lot of work to do, Max and I.

Determined to continue, with my ankle freshly bitten, I tried to re-engage Max. Max, still crawling under the table on all fours, said, "I'm so mean! *Roar!* Run away from me!" I peered down at him and offered, "You look like a nice dinosaur to me." He said, "No! Play *my* game. I'm mean, bad, and dangerous!" With my last breath of patience, I said, "Max. I have studied dinosaurs for many years. You have all the features of a nice-a-saurus." To my relief, Max giggled and got back in his chair and asked to see the blocks again.

As educators, we have all worked with kids like Max—kids who pull at our patience, push our buttons, and require a high level of support. I could have been more authoritarian with Max, demanding that he follow the rules, but there are many ways to reach students. Our job is to figure out what each child will respond to. In my experience, building an unconditional positive relationship with a child is the foundation for learning. I didn't get to work with Max as much as I would have liked. I was not assigned to Max's school, so I worked with him a few times and then shared with the teacher some strategies. That I thought might work with Max. And then I moved on to the next "Max."

Fortunately for me, a year later, when I was given another student to work with at his school, I got the chance to see Max in his second-grade classroom. At first I thought this child who looked like Max was Max's twin or something, because although he *looked* like my Max, he was a different child. He was sitting and listening attentively to a read-aloud about (of all things) dinosaurs. He raised his hand and asked the teacher,

"Where's the page about the nice-a-saurus?" The teacher looked perplexed and said she didn't know. But I knew. He was sitting on the rug.

THE BODYGUARD

Shawna Messina

I BELIEVE TEACHING IS like the saying "Everything I learned, I learned in kindergarten," except the saying is more or less "Everything I learned, I learned my first year of teaching." A teacher will never forget her first class, she will always believe it to be her "worst," and it will be the first time she realizes that she *can* make a difference.

I had a disastrous start to my first year. I truly believed I was being railroaded by the principal, and my room felt more like a detention facility than a classroom. My room was filled with kids the other teachers had shrugged off as "problem" students. In my fourth-grade class, I had an alarmingly large boy—he was eleven, soon to be twelve, and he beat me in height and weight.

Mark was a student who had previously "fallen through the cracks," and after only a few short weeks together, I realized Mark couldn't read.

Standardized reading test scores placed him in the thirtieth percentile, and he was reading fewer than forty words per minute. He basically looked like an eighteen-year-old but read like a first grader. It didn't take a genius to understand that Mark had behavioral problems not because he was a bad kid, but because he was avoiding the inevitable teasing.

In addition to the challenge of keeping Mark out of the principal's office, I had to provide reading instruction on his level without humiliating him. Without bruising Mark's ego, I was able to find material, usually from the first- and second-grade curricula, to modify my reading lessons for him. I placed him in a reading group of mostly girls because they were kind about his struggles and he didn't have to worry as much about protecting his reputation. He was driven by football, so I collected the sports pages, downloaded articles, and checked books out of the library for him. I love football myself, and I would watch the Cowboys game on Sunday so that on Monday morning Mark and I could review the highlights. He was unaware that by discussing the game, I was checking for his comprehension; he just enjoyed talking about football.

Mark was being raised by his father and stepmother. Thankfully, Mrs. Campbell was aware of Mark's academic issues, and we met early in the year to discuss his behavior. She and I shared the same concern: How was Mark able to fool his previous teachers and not be held back in earlier grades with the reading comprehension and fluency of a first grader? After our first parent conference, I began to document his progress, keeping samples of his work, and I notified the school's diagnostician about Mark's academic deficits. The diagnostician gave me a detailed STEPS (Student Tiered Educational Plan) intervention plan packet that was an inch thick and said that I would have to fill it out and provide Mark with six weeks of documented intervention before he could be considered for special education testing. I reviewed the packet and quickly began to understand how Mark had "fallen through the cracks" in previous years: The paperwork was tedious and repetitious, and if Mark moved during the STEPS process, it would start over again at his new school. With all of that in mind, I started the STEPS process anyway.

Mark had been sent to the office during the beginning of the year for a fight on the bus, and he was seeing the counselor to learn to control his temper. I had a couple of complaints from female students that Mark was bothering them at recess and during PE. Unfortunately, he had a reputation in my building for being a "bad" student, and it seemed the only place he didn't get in trouble was in the safety of my classroom. Students often make choices that are out of their teacher's hands, and Mark made the mistake of holding a girl down and putting his hand up her skirt. He had exercised this bad judgment on the school bus, and before the school day started, Mark was seated in the blue chairs outside the assistant principal's door. I was checking my school mailbox and was upset to see him sitting there so early in the morning. His face betrayed immediate shame.

"What happened, Mark? Did you do something wrong?"

His voice cracked and he could not bring himself to tell me what offense he had committed. My assistant principal gave me the bus infraction to read, and I was able to respond only with one question: "Why?"

He looked away, but I know he understood that I was very disappointed in him. I tried to hide my tears, knowing he wasn't going to get a pass back to class. For committing sexual harassment, Mark was sent to an alternative school for thirty instructional days, and I worried the gradual progress he had made would quickly diminish. I also was angry to learn that the documentation I had been collecting on Mark would have to start over when he returned to my school.

The tone in my class changed. Mark's classmates and I missed his presence; he was an obvious leader in the room. I wanted Mark to know he was missed and we were anticipating his return. The students would write letters and draw pictures for Mark, and Mrs. Campbell helped us to keep communication open by playing mailman. I kept Mark's locker and desk the same, although I gained students while he was gone.

During Mark's absence, I received a new student named Jon, who appeared to have a real chip on his shoulder. I was told that I would have a meeting with administration, the counselor, and his mom, which worried me because that was not the usual policy for a new student. We met while Jon sat in the hallway, and I was informed we were having an ARD (Admission, Review, and Dismissal), which is a special education meeting). I wasn't sure what to say or how to behave, since this was my first ARD experience. Jon's IEP (individualized education plan) stated that he had been deprived of oxygen at birth and that he had learning and cognitive disabilities that placed his IQ in the range of a toddler. He had a behavioral plan, but it was just a basic outline of how to handle his immature behavior.

His mother made a plea for help in the meeting: "Can you please help me? My son is violent, and he set his sister's crib on fire last week."

I remember trying not to look appalled as I realized that this was going to be my new challenge. The committee decided to test Jon to see if he qualified as emotionally disturbed. In the meantime, I was to follow his IEP and behavioral plan.

Jon's first few weeks were difficult. He struggled with routines and was very aggressive toward the other students. I held his hand during the transition, and his desk was close to mine at all times. He thrived during recess, and although I had to watch the contact during the boys' flag football game, he began slowly to fit in. There were occasional outbursts, where he would cuss or throw things, and he would exhibit bizarre behaviors for attention, such as blowing his nose and then eating the Kleenex. Every day was a struggle, but I did have hope that Jon was going to be successful and that he would make progress in my classroom.

I was pleasantly surprised when Mark returned motivated to learn. We gradually set goals for his behavior and grades, and with success Mark became even more of a positive leader in my classroom. I would tutor him before and after school, without the other students' knowledge, and Mark's confidence in reading grew. Mrs. Campbell and I began to develop a strong relationship, and she voiced her concerns again about Mark's reading level.

"I did try to have him tested at his previous school for special education. I'm pretty sure he's got a learning disability, the poor kid."

"I think so, too." Then I said, "What you need to do now is put your concerns in writing."

She followed through, and I turned in the completed paperwork to request he be evaluated. My frustration grew when I found out that it would take at least six more weeks to have him tested. I was beginning to feel that I had failed Mark, just like his previous teachers. I contacted Mrs. Campbell and told her that her voice was more important than mine, and she called the school weekly to see if Mark was being tested. With the two of us playing vocal advocates, Mark was finally tested. Eighteen weeks later, he was labeled learning disabled and would finally receive the services he so badly needed.

Just around the time I celebrated Mark's progress and success, Jon was labeled emotionally disturbed. Mark, who was the male leader in my classroom, tried to keep the peace and would volunteer to be Jon's partner or help him to read. Most of the time, I would work with both of them, but on this particular day I had a different small group. Mark was bigger than Jon, and for some reason, on this day Jon took Mark's presence as a threat.

"Stupid nigger!" he yelled.

Although Mark had been working on his temper, he was clearly upset. Then Jon pushed him, and my class erupted with the anticipation of a fight. I knew that if Mark fought, he would again be sent to the alternative school, and I knew that Jon might not be able to control his anger and walk away. Without thinking, I got between the two students, and Jon threw me over a desk. The fall only hurt my pride. I was embarrassed because I landed on my back and my skirt flipped up. Mark picked me up and protected me until an administrator could come in and physically remove Jon. My principal wanted me to write a referral for Mark, saying that he was involved in the altercation, but I refused. Since Jon was older than ten, I had to make out a police report, and unfortunately Jon was sent to a juvenile detention facility. I praised Mark for protecting me, but it was a bittersweet feeling watching Jon taken away in a police car. I was happy to have witnessed Mark rise above his anger and become a positive leader, but I was also saddened to realize that I could not help Jon's situation or make a difference in his life.

I know teachers are not supposed to have favorites, but Mark earned a special place in my heart that year, and I considered him my protector. I kept my part of the deal, and by the time our state standardized tests rolled around, Mark felt confident in his reading. With his classification as learning disabled, he received certain accommodations, including being able to take the test at a lower reading level. I set the bar high, and Mark took the test on the third-grade level. It was all the help he needed, and he was able to pass his state test. Not only was Mark successful for the first time in reading, his reading level increased by two grade levels in one year. When I received the test results, I took Mark into the hallway.

"I've got good news! You passed your test!"

This child who looked more like an adult than a boy began to cry. He hugged me, which then made me cry.

"Mark," I said, "do you want your results to be our little secret? Or do you want me to share the news with the class?"

He said, "I would rather you tell them. Not my score, just that I passed!"

Obviously, he wanted to receive praise from his classmates, and that was just fine with me. I didn't want him
to lose his reputation in the classroom as the tough guy,
so I let him go to the restroom to get himself together. I
announced his success when he returned, and the class
began to cheer. That one moment made the entire year
worth it, and I now hope for that moment each and every
school year, the moment when you know that you made
a difference. I have had many of these moments, but the
first will always be the most memorable.

ACKNOWLEDGMENTS

I NEVER READ THE acknowledgments in books. However, now that I am the one writing the acknowledgements, I see their tremendous importance in the life of a writer! It turns out, it takes a village to raise a book from an idea to an actual book you can hold in your hands.

First and foremost, a big thank you to Jennifer Parson, my dear friend and de-facto publicist, who encouraged me to write a blog for educators in the first place. When I started Notes From the School Psychologist Blog in 2007, I was writing into cyberspace mostly for my own enjoyment, and for the enjoyment of ones of tens of my teacher friends. I never thought that anything would come of it. Thank you to Kaplan Publishing for finding me in a sea of blogs and asking me to compile this anthology! I am honored that you took a chance on a new author and editor.

I also want to thank my parents, Ann and John, and my sister, Sammi, for being my first three blog fans and supporters. A special thanks to you, Mom—you were my first teacher and my inspiration for becoming an educator. Thank you for sharing your love of teaching with me.

Last but not least, I especially want to thank my loving husband, Steven, for his support and encouragement. Steven, I love that you still love me even when I stress about writing deadlines, worry about my students, and talk incessantly about my writing ideas. I truly could not have done this without you. I am truly blessed to have you in my life.

With gratitude,
Rebecca
Notes From the School Psychologist:
studentsgrow.blogspot.com

About the Editor

REBECCA BRANSTETTER, PHD, is both a clinical psychologist and a school psychologist in the San Francisco Bay Area. She writes about her experiences working with students in her blog, *Notes from the School Psychologist,* at *www.studentsgrow.blogspot.com*. She just finished editing *The Teachable Moment* and couldn't be happier that these stories will be shared with other educators.

About the Contributors

SHERI A. CASTRO-ATWATER, PHD, is an associate professor of school psychology at California State University, Los Angeles. She currently teaches courses in alternative assessment, counseling microskills, and applied developmental psychology, and is the founder of the SUCCESS counseling program in the Pasadena Unified School District.

DAMIAN BARIEXCA has worked in the New Jersey public school system for ten years, first as a high school English teacher, and currently as a school psychologist. He writes about education, technology, and school psychology on his blog, "Apace of" Change (*http://www.apaceofchange.com*).

ELISABETH BERKSON is a special education teacher in San Leandro, California. She is in her sixth year of teaching students ages (6–9) with special needs.

VALERIE BRAIMAH is the vice president of instruction at the Alliance for College Ready Public Schools. She is responsible for strategic management of the Alliance's instructional team, and for implementation of their College Ready Promise initiative. A former teacher, administrator, program evaluator, and educational consultant, Ms. Braimah has extensive experience in the areas of school reform, staff development and program evaluation. She has taught in both the elementary and high school levels in Oakland Unified School District and in two California charter high schools. Formerly the Chief Learning Officer for Insight Education Group, Ms. Braimah spent over five years providing teacher professional development, conducting school-wide academic program evaluations, and facilitating school and district reform across the country. Ms. Braimah has a master's degree in public policy from Johns Hopkins University, with a specialty in education policy and literacy program development.

KATHERINE A. BRICCETTI, PHD, works as a school psychologist and writer/editor in the San Francisco Bay Area. She holds an MFA in creative writing from the University of Southern Maine-Stonecoast program. Her memoir, *Blood Strangers*, was published in May 2010 by Heyday Books. Kathy can be reached through her website: *www.kathybriccetti.com*

ALISTAIR BOMPHRAY is a sixth year English and Journalism teacher in Hayward, California. He co-edits the education blog "Teacher, Revised" (*teacherrevised. org*) and is currently working on survival guide for new teachers called *Teacher, Revised: A Generation Y Guide to the World's Most Important Profession.*

LIN CERLES, PHD, is both an educational psychologist and a licensed psychologist in the San Francisco Bay Area. She works with students with special needs in private practice and at the University of California, San Francisco.

ERIKA CHILDS is a fourth grade teacher at an inner-city Las Vegas school. She loves adventures of all kinds, whether they are found in the great outdoors or in the wild world of the classroom.

MISS D is from Ohio and is in her fifth year of teaching. She recently completed her M. Ed. in literacy. In the past, she has taught in a school specifically designed for students with disabilities. Currently, she provides interventions in reading and math for struggling students at an elementary school. In order to protect the identity of her students, Ms. D wishes to remain anonymous.

SUSAN DEMERSSEMAN, PHD, is a psychologist working in schools and providing workshops for teachers and parents in the San Francisco Bay Area. She is currently completing a book that is a collection of her writing, including many pieces previously published in the *San Francisco Chronicle*, *Christian Science Monitor* and other newspapers and magazines.

TIFFANY GRIZZLE taught third and fifth grade in Austin, Texas before taking some time off after the birth of her second child. Currently, she lives in Colorado with her husband and two children and writes for *Search Parker Magazine*.

JILL HARE is the editor of TheApple.com, a Monster Worldwide online community for teachers. Before becoming the editor of TheApple, she was a public school music teacher for over a decade.

JAN HASLER received her elementary teaching degree from Loyola University of Chicago and went on for additional certification as a reading specialist. During her tenure in Atlanta, she felt especially enriched in the teaching of learning disabled children and writes about one such experience. Recently, she has worked with the Florida Center for Reading Research to revise the standardized reading tests for the state.

RANDY HOWE is the editor of *One Size Does Not Fit All* (also published by Kaplan), a collection of teacher stories addressing issues of diversity in the classroom. He is also the author of more than 20 other books and trivia card sets. Randy is in his sixteenth year of teaching special education and currently works at The Sound School in New Haven.

SAM JANEWAY works for the San Francisco Unified School District as a behavior consultant and a special educator. Prior to that, he worked with students with emotional disturbance for 13 years.

VICKI LAUTSCH is a middle school math teacher in Phoenix, Arizona. She works with gifted students, and focuses on building conceptual understanding of mathematics for all of her students.

SHAWNA MESSINA is a fifth-grade literacy teacher at Lowery Road Elementary. She has been teaching for ten years. Ms. Messina was the Outreach Communications Reading Chair for the Fort Worth Independent School District in 2008–2009 and won the district's Primary Teacher of the Year award.

PATRICIA RICCIO is an English teacher in Palm Springs, California. She works in a Title I school, where students need just a little more attention than most.

JENNIFER SCOGGIN, the creator of Mrs. Mimi from the blog "It's Not All Flowers and Sausages," is also the author of the book by the same name. After teaching for eight years in Harlem, Jennifer is currently a staff developer and freelance education writer. In her non-existent spare time, she is a sixth year doctoral student at Teachers College, Columbia University.

AMBER MACKENZIE TAYLOR is an early intervention special education teacher in the San Francisco Bay Area. She earned her bachelor's degree in Development Studies at the University of California, Berkeley, focusing on women and children's grassroots development projects in sub-Saharan Africa. She worked for several years as a mental health assistant, supporting children with severe emotional disturbance in a day treatment facility, before earning her Moderate/Severe special education credential at California State University, Sacramento. Ms. Taylor is in now in her fourth year teaching a pre-kindergarten and kindergarten special day class for children on the autism spectrum. She now holds both Moderate/Severe and Mild special education credentials, and is in the process of completing her Early Childhood Special Education certificate.

ROSEMARY TAYLOR has taught for more than 30 years in Early Childhood Education. She is the second to the oldest of 14 children and mother of 3. She is the lead teacher in a Northern California preschool.

EXCERPT FROM

IT'S NOT ALL FLOWERS AND SAUSAGES

by Mrs. Mimi (as created by Jennifer Scoggin)

AVAILABLE WHEREVER BOOKS ARE SOLD!

My name is Mrs. Mimi and I am a second-grade teacher in Harlem.

"Hi, Mrs. Mimi!"

When I tell people what I do for a living, I usually get one of three reactions.

REACTION #1: "Oooooo . . . little kids are sooooo cuuuuuute! I am so jealous! It must be so fun to color and sing all day."

This reaction tends to send me into a bit of a rage, compelling me to regale these individuals with an insanely long laundry list of roles that teachers must balance. I feel the need to inform them of the incredible amount of planning and thought that goes into our days and point out that, unlike those who work in an office, I must complete all my daily tasks while simultaneously holding my own pee for eight hours at a time. *Eight hours!*

REACTION #2: "If I could spend some time volunteering, I would definitely work with children like you do."

Ummmm, moron, teachers get *paid* because we work *insanely hard*. But that's cool, I know you're really online shopping all day in your air-conditioned cubicle and are just feeling incredibly unfulfilled and worthless. Just try not to take it out on teachers next time, okay?

REACTION #3: "Wow! You work there?! You're totally like Michelle Pfeiffer in *Dangerous Minds!*"

Okay. No . . . just no.

I won't even respond to those who immediately point out that it must be nice to have my summers off. I feel as if they should just be shot.

(Note: Before continuing to read, please begin humming a song you think of as fairly badass. I find that having my own soundtrack helps make me feel even more fabulous than I already am. I mean, don't all inner-city public school teachers have their own soundtrack that follows them around? And wear lots of leather? Yes? No?)

Okay. So now that we've gotten *that* out of the way. . .

If I could, I would scream, "I am a teacher!" proudly from the highest mountain, but high heels do not lend themselves to intense hikes. Nor do I lend *myself* to anything quite so outdoorsy. Plus, screaming from a mountaintop just seems so cliché. And when you're a teacher, let's face it, there's practically a jungle of clichés for you to fight through, hence the ridiculous reactions I receive from those outside of the world of education when I tell them about my choice of career. Like I said, I don't do outside and I certainly don't do cliché. Let's take a look at some of these awfully inaccurate teacher clichés and poke some holes in them, shall we? Because I don't see myself represented anywhere . . .

Well, first we have the stereotypical image of an elementary school teacher who loves terrible thematic sweaters, sensible shoes, and necklaces made exclusively from dried pasta products and Tempra paint. This teacher may also be sporting some sort of dangly thematic earring that may or may not blink. Perhaps she is brandishing a pointer as well. I think this teacher's soundtrack might include hits from artists such as Raffi. Fortunately, she exists mainly in the cloudy, and very delusional, childhood memories of the classroom held by many who seem to think they went to school in a Norman Rockwell painting or something. I resent this teacher on many levels. But perhaps what I find most insulting is she is portrayed as a smiling idiot who is completely void of any sort of sass. She's just so . . . well, I think the macaroni necklace says it all.

I teach elementary school and somehow manage to

dress myself every day without resorting to anything that can be purchased at the grocery store. In all honesty, I think of myself (and my school wardrobe) as pretty fabulous. And while I may not have a lithium-induced smile plastered on my face and Raffi blasting from my room, I do love my little friends. A lot. So much so, that I have a hard time leaving school at school and often hear myself continuing to talk about the adventures in my classroom long after my friends go home at 3. And, if I'm not talking *about* my students, I'm talking to other adults as if *they were* my students. Like at home with my husband, Mr. Mimi, I might find myself saying something like, "Honey, is that really where you want to leave your shoes? Do we want this to be a place where people have to worry about tripping over shoes left all over?" Yeah, I think it's safe to say Mr. Mimi loves (read: tolerates) this little habit of mine. I've tried to reform, but there's something about spending the entire day with 20 small people who quickly become more like a little family that makes it hard to leave it all behind in the classroom. I have never thought of teaching as just a job.